FIVE DECADES IN POLITICS

FIVE DECADES IN POLITICS

Sushilkumar Shinde

as told to
RASHEED KIDWAI

HarperCollins *Publishers* India

First published in hardback in India by HarperCollins *Publishers* 2024
HarperCollins *Publishers* India, Cyber City,
Building 10-A, Gurugram, Haryana – 122002, India
www.harpercollins.co.in

2 4 6 8 10 9 7 5 3 1

This edition published in India by HarperCollins *Publishers* 2025

P-ISBN: 978-93-6989-080-4
E-ISBN: 978-93-6213-749-4

Typeset in 12/16.3 Bembo Std at
Manipal Technologies Limited, Manipal

Printed and bound at
Saurabh Printers Pvt. Ltd.

HarperCollins *Publishers*, Macken House, 39/40 Mayor Street Upper, Dublin 1,
D01 C9W8, Ireland

For my daughter Praniti Shinde, who fills my heart with joy each day.
She is following in my footsteps with a sense of service and sacrifice,
and a deep commitment towards democracy, our country,
the Indian National Congress, Solapur and much more.

—Sushilkumar Shinde

Contents

SECTION IV
Entry into Politics

SECTION V
Foreign Visits and Reflections

SECTION VI
My Years as a Veteran Politician

SECTION VII
Mentors and Leaders

A Note
from Sonia Gandhi

I AM DELIGHTED to learn that Sushilkumar Shinde's autobiography is about to be published. I am sure that it will be a significant addition to our understanding of the political and social history of the past half a century and more.

His life has been a saga of struggle. He has faced numerous odds and resolutely overcome them to occupy a number of high positions, which he utilized diligently and purposively to make many enduring contributions. He has been a stalwart Congressman all the way through his long career, symbolizing the party's foundational values—especially of secularism, an abiding concern for the weaker sections of society, and social justice and empowerment.

What has struck me all through our association is the nature of his personality: Ever-smiling, always calm and unruffled, and with a great ability to always listen to different viewpoints and find a middle path in the finest Indian traditions.

I wish him all the very best of health.

Foreword

by Sharad Pawar

THE LATE 1960S and early 1970s were vibrant years of my political career. My mentor Shri Yashwantrao Chavan was looking for enthusiastic youths hailing from all corners of society, especially from the underprivileged, downtrodden communities of Maharashtra, who would strive to uplift these communities from their miserable condition.

Sushilkumar, a young police officer clad in khaki, first met me at Mr Lele's house in Mumbai. I could see a spark in his eyes, aspiring to something bigger than what khaki could offer. Our frequent meetings would fuel his aspirations to become a lawmaker rather than a practicing lawyer or contenting himself with the role of a law enforcement officer.

Soon, in 1971, an opportunity beckoned when the state assembly elections were announced. The Karmala assembly constituency was reserved for the SC category and I strongly recommended Sushilkumar's name for the candidature.

But my demand was not approved by the high command. The days of disappointment passed, and opportunity again knocked on the doors of his political fortune, with the unfortunate death of Tayappa Sonawane, the MLA from Karmala. Sushilkumar's patience paid off and in 1973 he was elected with a big margin to the assembly constituency.

Sushilkumar never looked back; he went on to excel in his political career. Of course, I strengthened his wings in early years of his career, but over time he soared high with his self-fuelled energy. The strengthening of his wings was not just for him to soar high but to allow him to fly freely with his own intuitions and intentions.

In 1980, the Progressive Democratic Front government in Maharashtra under my leadership was dismissed before completing its full term. Smt. Indira Gandhi had regained her lost ground with an emphatic win in the parliamentary elections, and consequently in Maharashtra the fear of the Central leadership prevailed over the faith in me. Most of my colleagues left me, and Sushilkumar was not an exception. But his parting ways to join another party didn't affect our relationship at a personal level.

For Sushilkumar, walking through the corridors of power was not arduous; he happily scaled the ladders with his ever-smiling countenance. His steadfast loyalty to the Congress high command paid dividends and he became the first Dalit chief minister of Maharashtra in 2003. There were of course a few difficulties in his exceptionally smooth political career: he encountered some potholes of defeat, was dethroned from the seat of the chief minister in Maharashtra and sidetracked from active politics. His appointment as the Governor of Andhra Pradesh was an unusual episode in his political career but he took up the responsibility without complain. He was handpicked to contest the vice presidential election and did so despite the knowledge that he would ultimately lose. He proved himself as one of the most loyal of Congressmen, a trustworthy lieutenant of the high command.

We worked together in the state and at the Centre. As the chief minister of Maharashtra, Sushilkumar successfully tackled the drought conditions during the year 2003-04. In 2013-14, excessive rains and floods caused massive damages in the Vidarbha region of Maharashtra. I toured to the affected districts and returned to Delhi with my own assessment of the situation. Sushilkumar as the home minister took an immediate decision to announce a relief package for the affected farmers and families. This is just one example of his commitment to the distressed people. He would always support my suggestions and decisions in any meeting of the Empowered Group of Ministers.

His stint as the Union home minister will be remembered for his daring decisions to bring a terrorist to the gallows.

Sushilkumar embodies Lord Krishna's mantra on how to address a challenging circumstance: 'He who responds to every situation with a smile and never reacts with anger is the one who wins.' I appreciate that even today, he extends his gratitude to me for helping him make the journey from khaki to khadi.

Author's Note

by Sushilkumar Shinde

IN HER MEMOIR, *Africa's Child*, author Maria Nhambu speaks about growing up as an orphan. 'I marvelled at the beauty of all life and savoured the power and possibilities of my imagination,' she writes. 'In these rare moments, I prayed, I danced, and I analysed. I saw that life was good and bad, beautiful and ugly. I understood that I had to dwell on the good and beautiful in order to keep my imagination, sensitivity, and gratitude intact. I knew it would not be easy to maintain this perspective. I knew I would often twist and turn, bend and crack a little, but I also knew that … I would never completely break.'

As a child, I too grew up under testing circumstances—though the challenges were different. I had lost my father early and, with no support from the wider family, my childhood was an extended period of extreme poverty. From relative affluence, when my enterprising businessman father was alive, our fortunes changed overnight. As if that wasn't bad enough, there was also the crippling burden of being born into a caste long consigned to the lowest rungs of the social hierarchy.

But adversity brought with it resilience. I was fortunate to encounter kind, motherly figures who eased my pain, and helped me process the abuse and the neglect. Faced with endless challenges, I learnt to adapt early in life and grew up as a tree that would bend with the wind but not break. Later, people from different walks of life, both prominent and not so well known, would help me overcome the barriers of social exclusion—recognizing and appreciating my perseverance, industry, plain living and commitment to the ideas of justice, equality and democracy. If people like Sonubai and R.V. Deshpande helped me in the initial years as I struggled to find my feet in a hostile world, Sharad Pawar, Y.B. Chavan, Indira Gandhi, Rajiv Gandhi and Sonia Gandhi would come as godsent angels to guide and mentor me. Now, in the winter of my life, I can say with a degree of satisfaction that I could live up to their expectations.

The story of my life, though at times complex, has no scope for any sort of pretence or showing off. Indeed, I would say, it lacks the gravitas to impress. As for literary merit, as an avid reader, I recognize that this book is not like the autobiographical works of more accomplished authors who had set as their benchmark the writings of people such as St Augustine, Jean-Jacques Rousseau, Benjamin Franklin and Henry David Thoreau. Another point I want to clarify at the outset is that my memoirs are not part of any political act or any attempt to create a controversy, but a humble and honest effort to tell the story of my life and explore my sense of identity.

Now, a word about how this book is structured. Readers will immediately notice that though this is an autobiographical account, it does not follow a chronological order. Rather, what I have tried to do is explain how I lived my life, not only in terms of the high offices I held—that of the chief minister, governor and Union home minister—but also how I found a deep sense of fulfilment in theatre, travel and reading. Looking back, I feel my days in the green room or on the stage played a big part in shaping my life. The theatre was the beginning of my natural unfolding, helping me overcome the gloom and stress of the early years of my life. In many ways, it saved me, moulded me into a confident speaker and, in the process, transformed my personality.

This autobiography does not contain any sensational revelations, scandals or gossip because such things do not align with my worldview. Those who have known me would vouch for the fact that I have always stayed away from politicking, backbiting, intrigue and vindictiveness, throughout my long political career. In fact, offhand, I cannot recall any enemies or contemporaries I disliked. If my contemporaries share similar sentiments about me, I would consider that one of the most significant achievements of my public life.

This book would not have taken shape without the active support of my friend and author, Rasheed Kidwai. His understanding of politics, particularly of the Indian National Congress, and easy-going nature helped wrap up many sessions in the most engaging and productive manner.

My personal assistant, Vijay Gholap, has been most attentive and helpful. Vijay meticulously kept a record of my writings, speeches and photographs, which came in handy when I finally sat down to write this book. I wish to express special thanks to Sanjay Nahar, Dilip Chaware and N.B. Ghodke, who have had a long association with me, and assisted me in writing of this book. A special word of appreciation for journalist Milind Ghatwai and Dr Bhalchandra Laxman Mungekar (economist, educationalist, former member of the Planning Commission and member of Rajya Sabha), who generously supported me with the historical context of the Dalit movement in Maharashtra and helped rekindle many instances of the past. Without all of them my memoirs would have been incomplete.

I am grateful to HarperCollins *Publishers* India and its editor, Swati Chopra, for readily agreeing to publish my memoirs.

Mumbai
17 July 2024

SECTION I

My Stint as Union Home Minister

1

Two Dramatic Incidents

AUTOBIOGRAPHIES, BY THEIR very nature, possess an element of incompleteness, and my story is no exception. But within the vast and complex overarching story of one's life, there are some stories that stand out—periods that define who you are. In my case, one such period was my stint as India's home minister. It was a turbulent phase in the country's contemporary history and tested me in ways drastically different from the challenges I faced when I held other positions in the Union cabinet. Whether I was a good home minister or not, history will decide. But for now, I would like to place the ball in the court of my readers, before the following chapters of this book take them further back or ahead.

After all, no story travels in a straight line.

Dates are important in any narrative. And in this one, 3 February 2013 stands out, marking a key moment in the country's response to terrorism and aggression on its sanctum of democracy. So I'll begin this account with that date, which also put me at the centre of events as the home minister.

That was the day President Pranab Mukherjee rejected Kashmiri terror suspect Afzal Guru's mercy petition, in what would be his second rejection of such a plea in less than three months—the first being that of 26/11 terrorist Ajmal Amir Kasab. For me, too, this was the second case of terror-related execution.

Both Mukherjee and I had assumed our new roles within a week of each other. While Mukherjee was sworn in as President on 25 July 2012, I took charge six days later, on 31 July, which meant both of us had to deal with such unpleasant matters quite early in our respective tenures.

Now let's come back to Afzal, who was convicted for his role in the December 2001 attack on the Indian Parliament. The date of his execution had initially been fixed for 8 February 2013 and then deferred by a day on the ground that the news of the hanging could lead to a law-and-order situation in the Kashmir Valley.

Typically, a hanging order involves a bureaucratic process that takes two to three days to complete. On the day Afzal was scheduled to be executed, we took a lot of precautions to ensure that the media did not get wind of it. Confidentiality and probity prevent me from disclosing any details, but this much I can say: We had informally worked hard to prevent any major repercussions in Jammu and Kashmir following the public announcement of Afzal's execution. If one recalls the violence in the Valley after the encounter death of militancy poster boy Burhan Wani in July 2016, my point would perhaps be better understood—about the potential consequences we aimed to avoid.

To maintain this secrecy, I held high-level meetings in my ministerial chamber where senior officers like Vimla Mehra, director-general of Tihar jail; R.K. Singh, Union home secretary (now a minister in the Narendra Modi government); and Sunil Gupta, the Tihar jailer, were present. I repeatedly enquired whether they were confident in their ability to carry out the execution even in the absence of a regular hangman.

Every decision we took was carefully considered and in keeping with the law of the land as the convict had exhausted all legal avenues, including appeals in the Supreme Court. It was only after the apex court's final decision that Afzal's file had been sent to the home ministry. Still, I have an admission to make: The Union home secretary's office was late in informing Afzal's family. This lapse, due to the home secretary's department's laxity, meant that his family could not meet him for one last time. But this much I can say: as far as I was concerned, there was no personal or emotional involvement in the execution.

Ajmal Kasab, as we know, was the sole surviving Pakistani gunman involved in the Mumbai attacks of 26 November 2008. He was hanged on 21 November 2012, a day before the winter session of Parliament opened. His execution marked the completion of the judicial process on the 26/11 attacks. We notified Pakistan about the hanging—first through a letter, which was not accepted, and then through a fax message. Our neighbour declined to accept the body.

Before I conclude this chapter, I would like to remind the readers that we, in the government, were not the punishing authorities; the punishment for Ajmal Kasab and Afzal Guru had been delivered by the courts. This is what Mukherjee observed in his memoirs, *The Presidential Years*, and I am tempted to quote our late President, as his words convey my own sentiments on the matter:

> The law of the land had to be upheld. While I deliberated long and hard over the files of mercy pleas, once I had taken the decision—even of rejecting them—I let the issue rest. I may have had sleepless nights while considering my decision, but after the decision was made, the matter was closed as far as I was concerned.[1]

So, that's that. I have dealt with two dramatic and difficult incidents during my tenure as Union home minister. It could have been anybody else in my place. I merely happened to be the home minister at the time and tried to do my job to the best of my abilities, in keeping with what was expected of a seasoned politician in a key post. But how did someone from an extremely humble background rise to hold such an important political post? The next chapter deals with that—and more.

---

1 Mukherjee, Pranab. *The Coalition Years: 1996-2012* (New Delhi: Rupa, 2017), 73.

2

'Saffron Terror'

31 JULY 2012 was a red-letter day for me. I became the country's home minister—an elevation I owe to Sonia Gandhi, chairperson of the United Progressive Alliance (UPA) and my mentor.

The Congress-led UPA was in its second term at the Centre. I had been the Union power minister for over six years when Sonia-ji called me one day. 'You have to take charge of the home ministry,' she told me.

I thanked her, noting that her decision was a testament to the opportunities the country provides to people from humble backgrounds. Having started my career as a police sub-inspector many years earlier, my appointment as the home minister of the country was a fitting tribute to our vibrant democracy and the political culture of the Congress party, which had always nurtured and promoted talent, ensuring social justice and equal opportunities for all. I also thanked Sonia-ji on behalf of the entire police force of the country.

Sonia-ji seemed amused and advised me to do good work to protect the security and sovereignty of the nation. Two hours later, I was officially told to take charge of the ministry at the majestic North Block. I was received at the gate by R.K. Singh, who was the Union home secretary then, and Bhanwar Jitendra Singh, who was the minister of state for home. That was my first entry into the North Block.

My first day in the ministry was spent understanding the work it did. It is a huge department, with nineteen secretaries from the civil services under my command, and I had to understand the functioning of all their subdivisions as well. I spent the second day with various departments, like the paramilitary forces, the Intelligence Bureau and the Central Bureau of Investigation, and was briefed by them. So, while day one was spent meeting the departmental heads and political persons, and getting to know everyone at the ministry, the real work started on the second day. This was also a time when violence and some wanton killings in Assam had sparked fury in cities such as Mumbai, Pune, Bengaluru and Hyderabad. In Mumbai, for instance, a protest had turned violent and led to large-scale arson. Two persons were killed in police firing and more than fifty were injured, including many policemen. I had to take quick and drastic action to restore peace and normality.

All the while, I was acutely aware of my origins as a sub-inspector, and it felt surreal to have so much power as the head of all the law enforcement agencies in the country. An avalanche of memories swept across my mind while sitting in the home minister's chair. I also whispered a prayer and remembered my illustrious predecessors such as Sardar Vallabhbhai Patel, Govind Ballabh Pant, Y.B. Chavan, Charan Singh, K. Brahmananda Reddy, S.B. Chavan, Zail Singh, P.C. Sethi and others. I familiarized myself with all the departments and made efforts to find out all the issues they were facing. And there were many issues in the Northeast at the time, such as violence and riots in Assam, Meghalaya and Nagaland, and I tried to figure out solutions. My experience as the All-India Congress Committee (AICC) general secretary in charge of some Northeastern states came in handy, and I was able to gain first-hand experience of political, ethnic and administrative challenges in the region.

It wasn't long, however, before I would be speaking openly on a very different type of challenge.

FINGER AT PARIVAR

In January 2013, I was at an AICC convention in Jaipur. Addressing the session on the final day of the *chintan shivir* (introspection camp), I spoke about 'saffron terror' and how the home ministry investigations had revealed that some saffron organizations were conducting training camps to spread terrorism. 'Reports have come during the investigation that the BJP and the RSS conduct terror training camps to spread terrorism ... Bombs were planted in the Samjhauta Express, Mecca Masjid, and a blast was carried out in Malegaon. We will have to think about it seriously and will have to remain alert,' I had told the AICC delegates. 'We have to take these facts seriously and remain alert.'

I had come across the term 'saffron terror' in one of the confidential papers prepared by the Union home ministry. But it was an issue that had the potential to snowball into a huge controversy since the Bharatiya Janata Party (BJP) and its ideological fulcrum, the Rashtriya Swayamsevak Sangh (RSS), were apparently involved. I was, therefore, careful to first check the veracity of the allegation before going public with it.

If anyone refers to my media statements from that time, they will notice that I carefully chose the term 'saffron terror'. I remember someone from the media had asked if it was Hindu terrorism or saffron terrorism. 'This is saffron terrorism [that] I have stated,' I had replied.

At one level, though, I was a little embarrassed about my remark because of its timing. The highlight of the day was Rahul Gandhi-ji making an important speech as the newly appointed vice president of the Indian National Congress (INC). But instead of focusing on Rahul-ji's emotional and inspirational speech, the media had highlighted my statement.

Subsequently, R.K. Singh also spoke, which was a pleasant surprise because it is rare to see an Indian Administrative Service officer dwell on politicized issues. I thought it was very courageous of him to do so. But one must remember that this officer from Bihar was involved in arresting L.K. Advani during the BJP leader's 1990 rath yatra.[2]

---

2 Manish Kumar, '5 years ago, he spoke of RSS' terror link. Now minister, his explanation', NDTV, 25 April 2018, https://www.ndtv.

In October 1990, when Advani entered Bihar, en route to Ayodhya in Uttar Pradesh in support of the Ram temple movement, then Bihar Chief Minister Lalu Prasad Yadav had asked Singh, who was the district magistrate of Samastipur, to arrest the BJP leader. According to anecdotal and media accounts from that time, Singh, along with a police officer, had shown up at Advani's room and informed him that they had been sent to arrest him. Singh, I may add, would later serve as a joint secretary when Advani was Union home minister in the Atal Bihari Vajpayee government.[3]

I vividly recall that shortly after I spoke at Jaipur, Singh was quoted as seconding my view on saffron terror: 'Yes, there is evidence [of men suspected of bombings having links to the RSS].'[4]

However, after joining the BJP, he would retract that statement. By then, Singh had retired from service. 'The term saffron terror was coined by [then] home minister Sushilkumar Shinde. I never used that term,' Singh would subsequently say. But he did not deny that during his tenure as home secretary, the

---

com/india-news/as-home-secretary-rk-singh-spoke-of-rss-terror-link-now-power-minister-he-explains-1842275.

3 Manish Kumar, 'RK Singh, who arrested LK Advani 26 years ago, takes oath as minister', NDTV, 3 September 2017, https://www.ndtv.com/india-news/rk-singh-who-arrested-lk-advani-26-years-ago-takes-oath-as-minister-1745415.

4 Kamaljit Kaur Sandhu, 'We have evidence of RSS men's links to terror acts, says home secretary', *India Today*, 22 January 2013, https://www.indiatoday.in/india/north/story/union-home-department-comes-out-with-evidence-on-terror-links-to-rss-152292-2013-01-21

Ministry of Home Affairs did investigate allegations that saffron groups were involved in several terrorist acts, including the 2007 Samjhauta Express bombings that left dozens of people dead and the 2006 Malegaon blasts in Maharashtra.[5]

Singh accompanied me on many ministry-related trips, including one to America, where I had gone to see how the Federal Bureau of Investigation (FBI) worked. He guided me through all these trips with valuable advice on what to ask and how to position myself. In 2017, Singh was sworn in as minister of state with independent charge of power, and new and renewable energy in the Narendra Modi government.

In my Jaipur speech, I had expressed concern over other pressing matters too, such as infiltration from Pakistan, insurgency in the Northeast and Naxalism. 'Infiltration is from Pakistan; insurgency is in some states in the Northeast; and Naxalism is another challenge. An environment is being created against peace, but my department will do its best to expose such nefarious designs,' I had said. My speech also highlighted how the Indian National Congress had given opportunities to people from Scheduled Castes (SCs), Scheduled Tribes (STs), Other Backward Classes (OBCs) and minority communities to rise in life. 'Our leader, Sonia Gandhi, gave me, a Dalit, an opportunity to become Leader of the House in the Lok Sabha and there are many names

5 Dev Goswami, 'Raj Kumar Singh: Man who arrested Advani, linked bombing suspects to RSS, now a BJP minister in Modi government', *India Today*, 4 September 2017, https://www.indiatoday.in/india/story/narendra-modi-cabinet-reshuffle-raj-kumar-singh-lk-advani-arrest-rss-link-bombing-bjp-minister-1031607-2017-09-03.

from SC, ST, OBC and minority communities who were made ministers and given other opportunities.'

DIFFERENT FROM MY PREDECESSORS

As home minister, my style of functioning was different from my predecessors who had served at the North Block during the UPA years. I had an open-door policy and anyone who wanted to could meet me. I also came up with solutions, which created a buzz, in New Delhi's corridors of power, about me being a good home minister.

P. Chidambaram is a highly intelligent man. While he tends to be a little aggressive, he always maintains his relationships with his colleagues and has a bunch of officers loyal to him. Shivraj Patil, too, is a good man, but many people tried to tarnish his image, which is perhaps why he had to leave the home ministry. When Pranab Mukherjee became the President, Chidambaram was made finance minister and the home minister's seat became vacant, leading to my appointment.

Reflecting on my time in the UPA cabinet in various capacities, I've come to realize that serving as a home minister is drastically different from holding other cabinet positions. This is because the home ministry is a critical department where decisions must be made swiftly. Any difficult situation needs to be brought under control as early as possible, and there is no room for complacency because matters can escalate very quickly. It takes round-the-clock, relentless hard work of hundreds and thousands of personnel to maintain law and order.

Yet, the ministry's work often is under-recognized as peace and tranquillity are taken for granted. By extension, the home minister's job too is a thankless one. Appreciation for the work done is scarce, and it often entails enduring abuse and criticism. One key responsibility of the job is maintaining cordial relations with state governments—usually with the chief ministers and their chief secretaries. For example, in the Northeast, we had a good rapport with states like Meghalaya and Nagaland, which allowed us to swiftly solve many tricky issues.

A home minister's job also involves a lot of hard work, sometimes through the night. I recall one instance where R.K. Singh and I had to fly to Hyderabad at two in the morning. At the time, the situation in what was then undivided Andhra Pradesh was quite delicate due to the ongoing disturbances over the bifurcation issue. Having served as the governor of Andhra for a little over a year, between 2004 and 2006, I knew that my presence there could help bring peace. Although my stint as governor was brief, I had tried polishing my Telugu, having learnt the language in my hometown, Solapur.

In some ways, Solapur is Maharashtra's—and possibly India's—most multilingual and multicultural city. This is primarily because of Solapur's geographical location. The southern part of the city is close to Karnataka and present-day Telangana. Being on the border, it accommodates a large diaspora of people from these states. So, when protests began in Andhra's Seemandhra region against the bifurcation of the state, I found the response quite natural. Wherever a new state is being carved out, such feelings are bound to arise.

On 13 February 2014, I piloted the Andhra Pradesh Reorganization Bill, 2014, in the Lok Sabha. Without going into the specifics, I can say that everyone in the party and in the UPA was on board for the bifurcation of Andhra Pradesh. Yet, the INC had to pay a price for it.

The division of Andhra Pradesh—in the wake of Telangana statehood agitation—by Manmohan Singh's government in 2014 did not bring electoral dividends for the Congress. The move cost the party dearly in both the Lok Sabha and assembly elections, as it was decimated in both the newly created state of Telangana as well as Andhra Pradesh. Our leader, Sonia Gandhi-ji, repeatedly asserted the claim that the Congress alone was responsible for making Telangana the country's twenty-ninth state. But we won just 2 of the 17 Lok Sabha seats and 21 of the 119 assembly seats. It heartens me to say that the people of Telangana finally acknowledged our sincerity and commitment when they gave us a resounding mandate in the assembly polls of 2023.

Many a times I am asked about my first impressions of Narendra Modi. As home minister, I did not have much interaction with the Gujarat government, then headed by Narendra Modi, who rose to become Prime Minister in May 2014. During the ten years of his tenure as PM, from 2014 to 2024, the economy got derailed, there was rampant unemployment, and efforts were made to pit one religion against another and whip up communal passions. It was both shocking and funny to hear Modi praise Solapur jackets during a campaign speech in Shirdi in 2014. Perhaps, he was not aware that those particular jackets are not made in Solapur.

A lot has also been said and written about the surgical strikes in 2019 when our Indian Air Force daringly crossed the Line of Control to destroy terror camps in Pakistan. Without getting into the specifics, I can share with confidence that during the UPA years (2004–2014), we too had carried out surgical strikes. When I was the home minister, our government brought down the number of terror camps from sixty-five to forty, but we never advertised our work. Surgical strikes are not meant to be made public, but the Modi government is used to marketing such events and it has benefitted from this, as was evident during the 2019 Lok Sabha polls.

Prime Minister Modi used military services, particularly the Indian Air Force (IAF) to score political points. Just as the 2019 Lok Sabha polls were set to commence, the Indian Air Force conducted a highly successful and clinical air surgical strike on Jaish-e-Mohammed's training camp in Balakot to avenge the Pulwama suicide bombing attack. Within days, Modi and the BJP began harping on its political benefits. The BJP election posters carried motifs of the Pulwama attack and IAF strikes in Balakot. Wing Commander Abhinandan, who was taken prisoner by Pakistan (but released two days later), also started figuring on election publicity material. We are all proud of our air force and armed forces, but the BJP projected military success as part of its Right-wing agenda, indulging in muscle-flexing and politicizing our defence forces.

NIRBHAYA CASE

I am not a strong believer, but I had prayed for the life and health of Nirbhaya, the twenty-three-year-old who was raped and brutalized inside a bus in Delhi, and who later died from the horrific injuries she had sustained. The 16 December 2012 case had numbed many, including me, into disbelief. All I can say here is that we tried our level best in terms of diligent investigation and enactment of pioneering legislation for a speedy trial and exemplary punishment. We were quick to track down the culprits. We also sent Nirbhaya to Singapore for the best treatment possible, but destiny had willed otherwise.

I tasted my first defeat in the next general election in 2014, when I was in the fray, for the first time, from a 'reserve' seat. There was a strong wave in favour of Narendra Modi. I accepted the defeat with humility and started working for people from the next day. Thereafter, I was not keen to contest in 2019, but the party could not get suitable candidate. Though the political situation was somewhat different this time, BJP still benefited from the division of votes. I announced my political *sanyas*; I would not contest another election in the future.

3

The Anna Hazare Movement and Other Events

THE EARLY YEARS of the last decade were a turbulent period in our country's recent history. When I took over as Union home minister in the later stages of the UPA's second term in power, the Anna Hazare-led movement, seeking the creation of a Lok Pal—an anti-corruption ombudsman—was in full swing. I must make it clear at the outset that the movement was uncalled for and proved extremely harmful to our government. We can see now why Hazare has gone so quiet. I have no hesitation in saying that the veteran social activist was used by the RSS–BJP combine effectively and that many members of the so-called civil society became willing tools in their nefarious designs. Several media reports and subsequent statements pointed at that direction.[6]

6 Shabbir Ahmed, 'RSS stage-managed Anna Hazare movement, says ex-India Against Corruption team member', The News Minute, 30 July 2023, https://www.thenewsminute.com/news/rss-stage-managed-

Incidentally, I was on very good terms with Hazare. While he was not so active on issues of national importance when I was chief minister of Maharashtra between 2003 and 2004, he did raise a lot of local issues at that time as well. Once, I had even visited his gram panchayat to address a meeting. There is an interview where Hazare has praised me, saying Sushilkumar Shinde is a good man who has done a lot of work for the state.

Since his India Against Corruption protests of 2011–12, Hazare has not done much, but he has often admitted in private that the movement did not pan out the way he had intended it to. I hope that some day he musters the courage to spell out how he was tricked by the Sangh *parivar*. Team Anna was split on the issue of forming a political party. While Anna Hazare and a few others did not want to enter mainstream politics, Arvind Kejriwal, who led the campaigning group, was very keen on it, and subsequently formed the Aam Admi Party in November 2012. The BJP would eventually storm into power in May 2014, riding on a potent cocktail of issues ranging from alleged corruption and economic slowdown to religious divisions. Eventually, it handed the INC its worst-ever defeat in independent India.

But throughout this fraught period for the UPA government, there was this constant buzz about a possible further elevation for me if the Congress-led alliance returned to power in the 2014

anna-hazare-movement-says-ex-india-against-corruption-team-member-180413; '"Kejriwal knew IAC movement was propped up by BJP-RSS," says Prashant Bhushan', The Wire, 15 September 2020, https://thewire.in/politics/prashant-bhushan-arvind-kejriwal-upa-iac-bjp-rss.

general elections. One media report in *India Today* said, 'If the Congress comes to power in 2014, despite reduced numbers, it could project Shinde as the Prime Minister.' It went on to say: 'It would help the Congress play the first Dalit PM card to garner support for Shinde. And Shinde, unlike Manmohan Singh, who stunned the Congress with his stand on the nuclear deal, will stick to the party line. Clearly, 10 Janpath checked all the boxes before elevating Shinde ...'[7]

The reports had little effect on me. Given my temperament as a dedicated party worker, or a *karmayogi*, I never give much importance to such speculation. Even when people of the stature of Kuldip Nayar would bring up the topic, I would smile and say nothing. My life's philosophy has been somewhat summed up by the late English singer Amy Winehouse, who had once remarked, 'Life is short. Anything could happen, and it usually does, so there is no point in sitting around thinking about all the ifs, ands and buts.'

One of the biggest examples from recent memory of 'anything could happen' is Barack Obama, who went on to become the world's most powerful man, overcoming difficult initial years. Speaking of the former President of the United States of America, let me share with you something Sonia Gandhi once told me—that reading Obama's autobiography, *Dreams from*

7 Krishna Kumar, 'Family retainer with Dalit card', *India Today*, 6 August 2012, https://www.indiatoday.in/opinion/krishna-kumar/story/family-retainer-with-dalit-card-sushil-kumar-shinde-112345-2012-08-04.

My Father: A Story of Race and Inheritance, she was reminded of me. It was a subtle compliment, so typical of Sonia-ji, and an acknowledgement of the long political journey I had covered. She even gifted me a copy of the book when she visited Solapur to lay the foundation stone of 2X660 MW power project.[8]

Obama's story is an inspiration for all and there were many, even in this part of the world, whose eyes were perhaps moist when the first African-American President of the US took the oath of office in January 2009. My story is hardly as inspirational as that of Obama's, but, looking back, it had its share of personally satisfying moments—although they would not always lead to positive results.

One such moment came in 2007. For nearly six months, my name had done the rounds as a probable candidate for the Indian President's post, unimaginable for a person who was once a junior policeman. Earlier, in the 2002 vice-presidential elections, I had given a tough fight to BJP veteran Bhairon Singh Shekhawat, who was the candidate of the ruling National Democratic Alliance.

In 2007, the other probable INC candidates for President, according to newspapers and television channels, were Dr Karan Singh, Shivraj Patil and Pranab Mukherjee. However, it was

---

8 The project, executed by National Thermal Power Corporation (NTPC), entailed an investment of Rs 6,500 crore, was spread over 1,700 acres, and included a Solapur Power Training Institute at the power plant site.

Pratibha Patil, whose name came up at the last moment, who would go on to become the President.

KEY ISSUES

Before I wrap up this opening section of my autobiography, I need to mention some of the tricky and important issues that our government—and I, as a representative of that government—had to deal with. As home minister, I had repeatedly offered to talk to Maoists without any preconditions. I visited Darjeeling on Bengal chief minister Mamata Banerjee's invitation to look into the Gorkhaland agitation and also held several meetings with Kashmiri leaders. I tried to build a consensus on the National Counterterrorism Centre (NCTC), a good idea that was blocked by some states in the name of federalism, especially by chief ministers of states ruled by the BJP.

My experience as Union home minister has given me a lot of insight into the different dimensions of national security and all the complexities involved. A vast and pluralistic country like India needs to have a mix of policies with respect to economic, political, social, strategic, military and diplomatic powers at its disposal in order to secure the interests of the country and its citizens. National security, in that sense, is much more than preservation of the state or protection of the territorial integrity of India. We need to take care of every institution and community, because the challenges to India's internal security come from many quarters.

I had read somewhere that nearly 50 per cent of our citizens are affected by threats that are not merely 'law and order' problems. These threats have an external dimension to them, which falsifies the conventional wisdom that internal security threats are caused mainly by internal sources.

While on this matter, I remember what Manmohan Singh had said once: 'India is unique and a land of contradictions.' These contradictions often interact and give rise to factors that contribute to internal security problems. What are these factors? Let me mention some of them: Poverty, unemployment, inequitable growth, resource distribution, corruption, the nexus between criminals, police and politicians in organized crime, lack of development, prolonged judicial process, poor conviction rates, caste, communal discord and hostile neighbours. The order is random and each of these issues can have an impact on the country.

A REPORT CARD

In the less than two years that I was at North Block, the UPA government did try to do a lot through legislative or other measures. We strengthened the Unlawful Activities (Prevention) Amendment Act (UAPA) in 2012 to provide special procedures to deal with terrorist activities. Its main objective was to empower relevant agencies to deal with activities directed against the integrity and sovereignty of India. The Act made it a crime to support any secessionist movement or claims by a foreign power to what India claims as its territory. Framed in 1967, the UAPA has been amended several times: in 2008, in 2012 and then in 2013. I feel sad to see how it has since been misused to curb civil rights and legitimate political dissent. That was never our intention.

Another measure the UPA adopted, and which too would later be misused, was the progressive legislation called the Right to Information (RTI) law. While some of the RTI activism addressed genuine concerns, there were instances that tried to paralyse the decision-making process, taking advantage of a system that lacked sufficient safeguards to defend decisions taken in good faith by the bureaucracy. Both Sonia Gandhi and Manmohan Singh repeatedly stressed the need for transparent governance, even as bureaucrats tried to resist 'file notings' from being made public. These 'notings' are brief handwritten observations by bureaucrats on the contents of files they work on. After 2014, I have noticed an uneasy—and rather disturbing and mysterious—silence in the RTI movement and a lack of transparency, particularly in the Central government.

Among the achievements I am proud of is our handling of the Northeast, a region that has always been dear to me. On behalf of the Central government, I signed a tripartite Memorandum of Understanding (MoU) with the Government of Assam and factions of the Dima Halam Daogah (DHD), an extremist group which operated mainly in Assam and Nagaland. We announced special packages and oversaw elections in Assam's North Cachar Hills Autonomous Council. In Meghalaya as well an agreement was reached with the Achik National Volunteer Council (ANVC), enhancing the autonomy of the existing Garo Hills Autonomous District Council in the state.

In Manipur, we worked out MoUs with three Meitei insurgent groups and a separate MoU with the United People's Party of Kangleipak (UPPK). Following these agreements, many militants surrendered arms and joined the mainstream. I count these as positive developments during my stint in the North Block. Needless to say, I had sleepless nights in June-July 2023 when Manipur was engulfed in ethnic violence.

As Union home minister, I also had the satisfaction of seeing a decline in Left-wing extremism. In 2013 alone, there was an impressive 28.48 per cent reduction in incidents of Naxalite violence. However, one particular incident in Chhattisgarh caused a lot of pain. I lost some of my party colleagues to a dastardly attack by Maoists on INC leaders who were returning after a political rally. The attack claimed twenty-seven lives, among whom were Chhattisgarh Congress President Nand Kumar Patel and his son, Dinesh; former Union minister V.C. Shukla; and Mahendra Karma, who was seen as the driving force behind anti-Maoist movements in Chhattisgarh. The leaders were ambushed inside a dense forest while returning to the state capital, Raipur. It was not just an attack on the Congress but a cold-blooded, calculated attack on democracy.

The BJP-ruled state, under chief minister Dr Raman Singh, remained completely clueless. I accompanied Prime Minister Manmohan Singh and Congress President Sonia Gandhi to a review meeting, where the chief minister could not offer any plausible explanation. There was a strong case for imposing President's rule in the state, but Sonia-ji felt that efforts should be made to restore normality first instead of politicizing the matter.

Later, the rebels issued a four-page media statement on behalf of the Dandakaranya Special Zonal Committee, CPI (Maoist), taking full responsibility for the attack and revealing that their aim was to punish Mahendra Karma, founder of the Salwa Judum, a militia consisting of local tribal youths who were trained, mobilized and deployed as part of the state government's counter-insurgency measures.

After the attack, we rushed more than 600 Central Reserve Police Force (CRPF) personnel, including the elite CoBRA anti-Maoist commandos, to sanitize and take control of the attack site. I had also immediately ordered a probe by the National Investigation Agency. By the time the agency submitted its report, the government at the Centre had changed.

Up north, Kashmir would remain largely peaceful through my tenure as home minister. I made several visits, interacted with local Kashmiris, and could sense that the Valley was craving for change, peace and prosperity. We started 'Udaan', a special industry initiative to train and upskill Kashmiri youths. Under this project, thirty-five public sector units (PSUs) and corporates such as NTPC, BHEL, BSNL, ONGC, HAL, Canara Bank, Wipro, TCS, HCL Technologies, Infosys, Bajaj Allianz and CMC would train more than 54,000 youths.

Like millions of my fellow countrymen, Kashmir lives and breathes in my heart. As Union home minister, I tried my level best to attend to every problem and hardship faced by Kashmiris.

In fact, I became the first home minister of India, since 1990, to have visited the iconic Lal Chowk, the epicentre of Kashmir politics, which has for long been a separatist bastion. In November 2012, I visited the posh Polo View city centre, in a private car driven by the then chief minister Omar Abdullah. There, I interacted with people and even shopped like any ordinary citizen or tourist. I bought Kashmiri suits, fruits and even had some ice cream that Omar bought for us. Since our Lal Chowk visit was unscheduled, we decided to tour the city while staying at the Nehru Guest House and took only one escort vehicle along. We did not keep the security officials in the loop. We later reviewed the security situation and also discussed measures to control infiltration with Omar Abdullah.

Throughout my visit, we ensured that minimal disturbance was caused to the public. This is perhaps why many, such as Sheikh Gowhar Ali, joint secretary of the Kashmir Chamber of Commerce and Industry, recalled my visit fondly in 2019 when then home minister Amit Shah visited Srinagar.[9] During Shah's two-day visit, the arterial Dalgate–Nishat Road around Dal Lake was reportedly shut, causing immense hardship to local residents and triggering snarls on several other roads.

Here, I am here tempted to quote former Research and Analysis Wing (RAW) chief A.S. Dulat. In his recent memoirs, he writes:

> India is gradually forgetting the likes of Shinde and Vajpayee but in Kashmir, they have not been forgotten. These were the kind of men, the kind of political leaders who held out hope to the Kashmiri. The Kashmiri has, from time to time, lived with hopelessness. Vajpayee gave them hope, Shinde gave them hope. Even Dr Manmohan

---

9 Muzaffar Raina, 'Valley contrasts Amit Shah heat with Sushil Shinde ice cream', *The Telegraph*, 27 June 2019, https://www.telegraphindia.com/india/valley-contrasts-amit-shah-heat-with-sushil-shinde-ice-cream/cid/1693266.

Singh—who believed in peace more than anyone I know—tried to continue the process but as the Kashmiri observed, nothing he did could fructify in the end and nothing came of his best intentions.[10]

As Union home minister, I also had the opportunity to travel to many forward areas along the borders with Pakistan, China and Bangladesh. I must salute our brave soldiers and members of various paramilitary forces who keep round-the-clock vigil to keep the country safe and secure. No words are enough to describe their selfless service on such inhospitable terrain.

That sums up my stint as the country's home minister. I have tried to cover most aspects of my tenure and be as candid as possible. Was I a good home minister? I don't know. That's for the future generations to judge. All I can say is that it was an interesting period in India's recent history and I was right there in the thick of it all.

I also don't know whether I have succeeded in holding your interest, dear reader, but if you have come this far, I would consider it a privilege. For now, I'll go back nearly ten years to another phase of my life—as chief minister of Maharashtra. The next section of this book is about that period, from January 2003 to November 2004.

---

10 A.S. Dulat, *A Life in the Shadows* (Gurugram: HarperCollins *Publishers* India), 215.

SECTION II

Chief Minister of Maharashtra

4

In Mumbai's Hot Seat

IT WAS A January afternoon in 2003 when I got a call from my party leader, Sonia Gandhi. I was a member of Parliament and still had more than a year and a half left to complete my five-year term. But Sonia-ji had other ideas. She wanted me to take over as the chief minister of Maharashtra, where the Congress was in an alliance with Sharad Pawar's Nationalist Congress Party (NCP). I had always been a loyal party worker and my leader's wish was my command. And that was how I took over as chief minister from Vilasrao Deshmukh, who happened to be a good friend of mine.

Sonia-ji's decision came at a time when the INC–NCP alliance was going through an uneasy phase. There were media reports of some trouble within the Congress and over Deshmukh's handling of the NCP. It is important to remember that the alliance and the formation of the Democratic Front government had come within six months of Pawar breaking ranks with the Congress and forming the NCP over the issue of

Sonia-ji's foreign origins—a needless controversy that had hurt and angered every party worker, including me.

The Maharashtra Congress Legislature Party welcomed me, but the NCP took its time to declare its support. After a series of meetings, the NCP finally placed a condition that appeared to be impossible to fulfil. It wanted the powerful Maratha leader, Vijaysinh Mohite-Patil, to be appointed deputy chief minister. Patil and I both belonged to Solapur district, and many thought that some spokes would stop the wheel. But the Congress high command wanted me to become the chief minister at any cost and accepted the condition.

It was a tricky situation that called for diplomacy rather than insistence on protocol. So, prior to my election as leader of the Congress-NCP legislature party, I called up Patil to tell him that I would come over to his residence for a chat. I chose to meet him to ensure that there was no misunderstanding within the district, where the political pulse rate had already increased. It was the first time someone from Solapur was becoming chief minister. After the customary exchange of pleasantries, I told Patil that I would like him to join the government as deputy chief minister. He pretended to be a tad reluctant.

On 18 January 2003, I became the first Dalit chief minister of the state, an honour whose credit should rightly go to Sonia Gandhi. Governor Mohammed Fazal swore me in as Maharashtra's twenty-second chief minister in a simple ceremony at the Raj Bhavan in Mumbai. My name was cleared and finalized just two days before I took oath. Governor Mohammed Fazal delayed the swearing-in for two days on grounds of him being in Goa, even though the flying time between Panjim and Mumbai is barely an hour.

On the day of my swearing-in, outside the Raj Bhavan, thousands of my supporters from various districts from Solapur, Sangli, Ahmednagar, Osmanabad, Pune and Mumbai celebrated with slogans, sending ripples of excitement through the air. The crowd also cut across communities and castes as OBCs, Dalits, STs, Muslims and women joined in the celebrations, as if it was their personal triumph.

Just before I took the oath, my eyes fell on one man sitting in the front row. It was former President K.R. Narayanan, India's first Dalit head of state. Words can't describe what I felt.

IMMEDIATE CHALLENGES

When I took over, the state was reeling under a drought, the ever-increasing burden of loans, prolonged power cuts and caste conflicts. The Opposition was very aggressive and the party machinery was failing to perform.

After I was sworn in, I called a meeting of top IAS officers at the Mantralaya and asked them candidly: 'How has Maharashtra come to this situation when the best administrative brains in the country like you are around? We are colleagues and must change this picture.'

I was determined to salvage the situation. My day would start at the crack of dawn and end after midnight. I toured the state extensively, speaking with common people and holding discussions with officers at every level. All the while, a roadmap to pull Maharashtra out of the difficult situation was taking shape in my mind. I decided to introduce some drastic measures, such as tightening the economy. The first Maharashtra budget under me was widely admired. It was called a 'social justice budget' and envisaged deliberate steps to provide justice to the deprived segments of society. A novel feature of the budget was to extend financial assistance to bright students for higher studies abroad, provided they were socially and economically backward.

In the first year alone, ten students, including four girls, went abroad with the help of the Maharashtra government. I felt happy that I was able to achieve all this and much more in just a year.

During a presentation I made on this budget, at a conference of Congress chief ministers at Shimla, where Sonia-ji presided, everybody praised my efforts. I returned to Mumbai with renewed vigour.

'*DO HANSON KA JODA*'

Earlier in this chapter I spoke about my friendship with Vilasrao Deshmukh. Indeed, I wouldn't be exaggerating if I said it was a rare kind of friendship, especially in politics. In Maharashtra, Deshmukh and I were described as '*do hanson ka joda*', or a pair of swans, often used as a symbol of faithfulness in literature and in popular culture. So, the expression '*hanson ka joda*' to refer to our friendship meant a bond of togetherness and an identical sense of purpose. Because of our genial nature, we would also be called *hansmukh*—the *hans* being a reference to my jovial nature and *mukh* a reference to Deshmukh.

I made many friends during my long career, but my friendship with Deshmukh was exceptional. We had both emerged on the political horizon of Maharashtra soon after entering politics, though I was elected directly to the Assembly and Deshmukh started at the village level as head of a gram panchayat. Our friendship grew when Deshmukh too entered the Assembly. Deshmukh and I would interact often because we were both members of the council of ministers. In 1985, we both were mentioned as contenders for the top-most political job in the state. To the amazement of the high command, we would recommend each other's name to observers every time there was a prospect of electing a new leader.

'If you want a candidate from the Maratha community, consider Vilasrao,' I would tell the observers.

'Choose Shinde if the party wants a Dalit CM,' Deshmukh would advise the emissaries from Delhi.

The result was that neither of us was recommended for the job till 1999, when Deshmukh became chief minister for the first time. I followed four years later.

One afternoon, in January 2003, I entered Sonia-ji's 10, Janpath residence in Delhi, having been called on by her. I was not aware that something important, or a big office, was in store for me. It hadn't even occurred to me though the Congress central leadership had dispatched three AICC observers—Vayalar Ravi, Ghulam Nabi Azad and Pranab Mukherjee—to Sahyadri Guest House at Malabar Hills, Mumbai, to ascertain the political situation in the state.

In my naivete of sorts, I had taken along a good friend of mine, journalist Suresh Bhatewara, who came to see me just as I was leaving for 10, Janpath. After meeting Sonia Gandhi, I remained calm. On the way back, Bhatewara and I got talking but I feigned ignorance over the impending developments in Mumbai. However, Bhatewara proved to be a mind reader of sorts. The next day, the *Maharashtra Times*, a prominent Marathi newspaper, put out a headline announcing that I would be the chief minister of the state.

The transfer of power was smooth and cordial. Deshmukh was the first to wish me, while I promised to carry on the good work he was doing. Twenty-one months later, when I handed over the baton to him, after the 2004 October elections in Maharashtra had resulted in another lease in office for the Congress–NCP coalition, Deshmukh would smilingly promise to carry on the good work I had done.

By the time I reached home after the Vilasrao Deshmukh ministry had been sworn in, another assignment was waiting for me—a stint at the Raj Bhavan of what was then undivided Andhra Pradesh. But more on this in another chapter, where I have dealt with my days as a governor. For now, I'll focus on the time I was chief minister of Maharashtra, my successes and disappointments, and coping with the vagaries of politics.

5

Achievements and Letdowns

IN A SERMON given by Frederick Lewis Donaldson in Westminster Abbey, London, on 20 March 1925, the Archdeacon of Westminster had talked about seven social sins:

- Wealth without work
- Pleasure without conscience
- Knowledge without character
- Commerce without morality
- Science without humanity
- Worship without sacrifice
- Politics without principles.[11]

While we continue to observe the lofty and ideal principles of democracy, we also practise something that comes in the category of 'politics without principle'.

11 Charles Hoffacker, 'The Anglican origin of the seven social sins', *The Living Church*, 1 December 2022, https://livingchurch.org/2022/12/01/the-anglican-origin-of-the-seven-social-sins/.

It pains me to record here that some of my party colleagues, claiming to represent a particular caste, worked against me behind the scenes, making my caste an issue, despite my appointment as a Dalit chief minister having a positive, trickle-down impact. I had also stewarded the storm-tossed ship of the Congress-led coalition in the tumultuous lead-up to the October 2004 Assembly elections.

Earlier that year, in the (Lok Sabha) parliamentary elections held in May, the Congress had won thirteen of Maharashtra's forty-eight parliamentary seats. The NCP's tally was nine seats. Sonia Gandhi and Sharad Pawar had both attended a rally at Solapur, the two leaders sharing the dais for the first time since 1999, when the strongman from Maharashtra had parted ways with the Congress over Sonia-ji's foreign origins. The rally was attended by nearly 1.5 lakh party workers and voters from near and far—including Akluj, Mangalwedhe, Malshiras and Pune, some traveling over 200 kilometres to attend this rally.

In her speech, Sonia Gandhi made an important point about the need for alliances, clarifying that the Congress had teamed up with the NCP to 'save the country and secularism. It is not an opportunistic alliance like the NDA [National Democratic Alliance].'

But the October elections in the state five months later would be difficult for the coalition, in the aftermath of the severe drought that had affected large swathes of Maharashtra. The monsoon had failed that year and we had to declare a drought situation in eleven districts, namely Pune, Satara, Sangli and Solapur (in the Pune division); Nashik and

Ahmednagar (in the Nashik division); and Beed, Latur, Dharashiv, Jalna and Aurangabad (in the Aurangabad division). Seventy-one talukas in these eleven districts had been seriously affected by the drought.

My government had accorded top priority to fighting the drought. In some districts of the Marathwada region, including Nanded, which had received less than 50 per cent of the rainfall it normally receives, work had been provided to the affected people under employment-generation schemes.

I must mention here that despite requests for Rs 1,700 crore to be issued by the Centre as drought relief, the NDA government had sanctioned only Rs 41 crore. After the UPA came to power in May 2004, Prime Minister Manmohan Singh released Rs 201 crore in addition to 3 lakh tonnes of foodgrain. He and Sonia-ji visited Amravati, Nagpur, Satara and Solapur to review the situation. When Sonia-ji visited the drought-affected areas, she saw how my government had even arranged for fodder and water for cattle. We also had food-for-work programmes in place.

Despite this, quite a few farmers had died by suicide, unable to cope with the mounting burden of debt. It was one of the gravest challenges I had faced in my life and nearly every political analyst had written off the Congress-NCP combine ahead of the Assembly elections.

Apart from this, there was the problem of long and frequent power cuts. I had taken a considerable risk by deciding to supply free electricity to around 25 lakh farmers because the decision would saddle the government with an additional burden of

Rs 400 crore in every quarter. Another equally important decision taken by my government that helped turn the tide was to revive the Maharashtra Debt Relief Act. The Act prohibited private moneylenders from recovering loans they had given to farmers. My government also decided to write off Rs 345 crore in interest on crop loans taken by farmers.

While touring Maharashtra or speaking in the state legislature, I would invariably tell the Opposition—the Shiv Sena and the BJP—that running the state was a collective responsibility and not that of the government alone. The masses appreciated this stand, but the media did not notice it. The Opposition blamed my government but did not provide any solution to end the crisis. When the October elections were held, the electorate delivered what was basically a fractured mandate.

CAST(E) OUT AFTER VICTORY

The NCP won 71 seats, the Congress 69, the Communist Party of India (Marxist) (CPI[M]) 3, the Peasants and Workers Party 2, and Independents 7, taking the Democratic Front's tally to 152 in the House of 288.

When the election results were announced on 14 October 2004, it was clear that the NCP would stake claim to the chief minister's post, having emerged as the single-largest party in the House. I told the high command that the actual strength of the Congress, including the three seats it had left for the CPI(M), was one seat more than what the NCP had won. I had myself offered a seat in Solapur district to the CPI(M) and, after the elections were over, Sitaram Yechury had gone on record extending support to me. That meant I had the backing of seventy-four legislators, since the Peasants and Workers Party too had committed its support to me.

I was all set to head the state government again. But that was not to be.

When the NCP elected R.R. Patil as its leader, the Congress central leadership was led to believe that a tough chief minister would be needed to handle a strong Maratha satrap like Patil. My opponents had succeeded in convincing our party's observers from Delhi that if a Maratha leader was not named the chief minister in my place, the community would switch loyalties to the NCP. Therefore, to keep the NCP in check, the Congress thought it had to name a Maratha chief minister. This argument my opponents came up with—to remove me from the post—came as a shock to me, because not only had I functioned well as chief minister, but I had also steadied the sinking Congress ship in Maharashtra. It was ironic, I felt, that my caste would become a hurdle after I had helped the party do well. But I accepted the leadership's decision to replace me with my good friend Vilasrao Deshmukh without any hesitation. I would later learn that many of my party colleagues, influenced by forward-caste considerations, had lobbied against me. But I bear them no grudges, though it pains me to relive these memories.

So Deshmukh became the chief minister again. Within the hour, I was appointed the governor of Andhra Pradesh, and I moved there the following month, in November 2004. I would remain there till January 2006. It would be the first of several roles I would take up over the next ten years.

FAST FORWARD TO 2014

When the 2014 Lok Sabha elections were held, I was the leader of the House. We had expected the ruling UPA to be re-elected but the Narendra Modi–led BJP would go on to storm to power at the Centre. I was among those who lost, as the Congress plunged to its worst-ever defeat in national elections.

I had done a lot of work in Solapur, but that didn't stand a chance against Modi's powerful oratory and the rising popularity of Hindutva. I was confident of victory; however, the verdict on 16 May 2014 left me stunned: I had polled 3,68,205 votes while my rival, Sharad Bansode of the BJP, got 5,17,879. I was hoping to romp home on the back of the strong roots Congress had had in Solapur and my own public standing.

In 2019, the BJP fielded a new entrant—Jai Siddheshwar Shivacharya Swami, a Lingayat seer—and then there was Prakash Ambedkar, who was the president of Bharipa Bahujan Mahasangh and had founded the Vanchit Bahujan Aghadi (VBA). This made the election a three-way contest.

The VBA comprised various SCs, STs and Dhangar groups, giving Prakash Ambedkar a strong support base in my constituency. Moreover, his chief ally was the Asaduddin Owaisi-led All India Majlis-E-Ittehadul Muslimeen (AIMIM), which also deprived me of some votes belonging to Muslims who had been voting for me all along. As a result, Prakash Ambedkar managed to take away 1.3 lakh to 1.45 lakh of my votes.

Swami was reportedly from the Swami caste (an upper caste group), but since the Solapur seat was reserved at that time, he filed his documents stating that he belonged to a Schedule Caste. There is an ongoing case against him that he hid his upper caste status to be able to contest from Solapur.[12]

The back-to-back electoral defeats of 2014 and 2019 were most hurtful. As my favourite leader Abraham Lincoln had succinctly remarked, 'The ballot is stronger than the bullet.' Even as I dejectedly said goodbye to electoral politics, I kept thinking about the voting behaviours of our countrymen—because voting is also an expression of our commitment to ourselves, one another, our country and the world. 'Elections,' as Lincon had said, 'belong to the people. It's their decision. If they decide to turn their back on the fire and burn their behinds, then they will just have to sit on their blisters.'

12 'Solapur BJP MP's caste certificate declared invalid: Bombay HC grants interim stay on panel's decision', *The Indian Express*, 12 March 2020, https://indianexpress.com/article/india/jaysiddheshwar-shivacharya-mahaswami-solapur-bjp-mp-caste-certificate-bombay-hc-6310872/.

SECTION III

My Origins

Every time I pick up autobiographies of famous people, I have the same feeling of awe. *How well they have structured the story of their lives. How easily the narrative flows.* And then I wonder how they figured out the perfect beginning and the perfect ending. It couldn't have been easy. No, certainly not. I suppose it's the beginning that is the most difficult part. Where to begin? How do you introduce yourself to the reader? And, after you have introduced yourself, what next? How do you proceed, while keeping the reader interested in the story of your life?

It's mind-boggling but, in the end, I went by what Graham Greene says: 'A story has no beginning or end: arbitrarily one chooses that moment of experience from which to look back or from which to look ahead.' I chose the two most important phases in my political career to begin this story—as the country's home minister and as chief minister of Maharashtra. The two roles would define my life in the sense that they would test my character, abilities and resilience, especially for someone whose early years were spent battling the twin disadvantages of a socially underprivileged birth and economic hardship.

Still, I believe, I have managed to do well for myself but a big share of the credit for that goes to my upbringing. This section is about that part of my life—my origins and my childhood. The first chapter of this section deals with my roots. The second talks about my life as a young man 'impatient to assume the world', to borrow T.S. Eliot's words.

6

A Humble Beginning

MY FAMILY TRACES its roots to Paranda *taluka* in Osmanabad[13] district of the Marathwada region in present-day Maharashtra. My great-grandfather, Rano-ji, was a typical Indian. He believed in leading a simple life and meekly accepted the prevailing social structure as it had existed for centuries. Menial jobs and serving the higher castes were part of his creed, and he never grumbled about the social milieu that treated him and others of his ilk worse than cattle. Changing the situation or aspiring for success was beyond the imagination of people like my great-grandfather, whose highest ambition in life was to get two square meals a day by discharging the duties society had imposed upon him. It would be unfair to blame him, or others like him, for not rebelling, since the circumstances were not conducive to any such attempt.

---

13 Osmanabad has been renamed Dharashiv, but the renaming has been challenged in a court.

Although the India of those days was dreaming of freedom, the winds of political activism had not touched the Marathwada region, which was under the rule of the Nizam of Hyderabad. Most Hindus found their religion a disadvantage because the Nizam was a Muslim, but it was significantly worse for those who belonged to the lower rungs of the social hierarchy. Needless to say, the caste system was inflexible here.

The Dhor caste, to which my family belonged, typified this abominable social injustice. It was among the lowest castes, whose traditional occupation was to cure the skin of dead cattle and sell it for making leather goods. While my great-grandfather accepted the disadvantage he had inherited by virtue of his birth as something inevitable, my grandfather, Shivram, was made of sterner stuff. He had come of age when the freedom movement was sweeping through British India and realized that his prospects in the princely state—with its oppressive social system—would be limited. So, he migrated to Solapur town, believing that his caste would not come in the way of a better future.

But the initial years wouldn't be easy. Although skilled and ambitious, my grandfather could not get out of the social ghetto he was trapped in, even in urban Solapur, and had to follow in the footsteps of other members of his community. He lived in Dhor Gali (lane), surrounded by the people of his community, speaking the same language and sharing the same lifestyle. My grandfather would tour the villages around the town, buy skins of dead cattle and cure them, but the traditional job brought him little income. He decided to diversify and started making leather bags, a novelty in the small town. Soon, he came to be known as a master craftsman.

Later, he started using sheepskin, which was cheaper, easier to cure and better suited to make durable bags. The demand for bags increased rapidly and, with it, his income. His achievement was extraordinary, given his social status, and his reputation reached Mumbai where his bags captured a niche market in the country's commercial capital. By the time my grandfather died, a prosperous business line had been firmly established.

My father and two uncles continued the business of making and supplying bags to traders in Mumbai. Mahatma Gandhi was among their numerous admirers. He complimented their originality and would go on to write to them, appreciating their work as promoting the concept of Swadeshi. Our family treasured the letter.

My father, Sambhajirao, like his father, took a bold step. He had been feeling for some time that his growth and success had been hampered in a joint business, and was confident that he would prosper more if he worked on his own. So, one fine morning, he announced his decision to separate from his two brothers to start his own business.

As the sole owner of a thriving business, he became affluent. He was fond of the good things in life but the joint family structure had restricted his options. Now that he was on his own, he started enjoying good food at home and other comforts. But he was not content with just living a life of relative affluence. In those days, the hallmarks of wealth were owning land, a house, and cattle and cart. My father decided to announce to the world that he was now a successful businessman, economically liberated and free of the social restrictions that had stifled him as just another resident of Dhor Gali. So, he built a bigger house, which stood out in the poverty-stricken locality.

While Sambhajirao's wealth made him a community leader, something remained missing. He longed for a son. When his first wife did not conceive, he married again. He married two more times, in between trying to propitiate every god in Solapur and elsewhere. When his third wife, Krishnabai, did not conceive, she asked him to marry her younger sister, Sakhubai—my mother. Sakhubai's first three children did not survive long after their birth. Finally, on 4 September 1941, my father's prayers seemed to have been finally answered, and I was born.

I was named Dnyaneshwar, after the thirteenth-century saint-poet revered across Maharashtra. Although a popular name, many found it difficult to pronounce. Everybody, including my family members, started calling me Genba. This name would later be discarded, and I would eventually take a new name, Sushilkumar. But more on that in the next chapter.

In keeping with a tradition that required naming a child with a lowly name to ward off evil forces, I was also called Dagdu (a stone). Names like Dagdu and Dhondu, which both mean the same, are common across Maharashtra.

TRAGEDY STRIKES

On 15 July 1947, my life turned upside down. My father died, leaving behind a family unused to the ways of the world. Friends vanished, the business collapsed, and a day came when there was no one to support my mother and stepmother. Used to affluence and material comforts, my family turned poor almost overnight. Relatives and acquaintances expressed their sympathies, but no one offered a helping hand. For days, my family grieved alone.

Our family had no savings. My father never kept records, and those who had borrowed money from him had long vanished. The only way to run the household was by selling off the family gold. Once that was exhausted, my mother and stepmother somehow survived by doing household chores for others.

With both mothers lost in their grief, there was no one to counsel or comfort me. I was devastated, unable to grasp the abrupt transformation in fortunes. I started keeping bad company and rarely attended school. Eventually, I failed my fifth standard exam.

Unknown to my mother and stepmother, I continued to lead a vagrant lifestyle and soon became adept at petty theft, selling the daily pickings to satisfy my craving for good food, which was no longer available at home. Along with a few like-minded friends, I formed a gang that specialized in lifting wares from pavement vendors. Eating sweets and watching movies with the ill-gotten money became our favourite pastime. While I soaked in the illicit pleasures of this freedom from strict parental supervision, my mother continued to try, in vain, and inculcate some values in me by narrating tales from the scriptures.

But a day would come when this life too would change. I remember it vividly, as if it was just yesterday. A woman who sold trinkets on the pavement had gone somewhere and I had stolen from her thinking nobody had seen me. But a couple of vendors from the opposite pavement saw me running away and told the woman when she came back that a fair-skinned boy had lifted something. I was the only one matching the description of the suspect and the vendor reached my home. By then, I had already sold the trinkets to a pawnbroker. My mother refused to believe the vendor. She said that her son could never stoop so low and scolded the vendor for levelling such an allegation against a child. The vendor, choking back her tears, turned to me and said, 'I thought you were a good boy.'

After the vendor left, I felt miserable. My mother must have noticed my guilt-stricken face and slapped me hard. She then dragged me to another room where we had idols of different deities and made me stand before them.

'I want to know what happened,' she told me. 'And don't you dare lie before the gods.'

I had no option but to confess. My mother made me lead her to the pawnbroker. She paid him the two rupees he had given me, reclaimed the trinkets and took me to the vendor to return the items in full public view.

My humiliation was complete, but my mother had taught me the most valuable lesson in life. After we returned home, she made me stand before the deities again and make a promise: I would never steal, whatever the circumstances. I have kept that promise.

I gave up thieving, but the craving for tasty food still had a strong pull. Spending our time around cinema halls, my friends and I hit upon a new idea to satisfy both our hunger and craving. Since we couldn't afford to buy and eat tasty food, we started looking for wrappers tossed away by customers leaving a sweetmeats shop. We would then pounce on the discarded wrappers and lick them dry.

One day, a shopkeeper caught me doing this. He scolded me, reminding me that my father was a rich man who used to feed others, and said that I should be ashamed of behaving like a beggar. Had he slapped me, I would have most likely brushed aside the temporary embarrassment and gone back to doing the same thing. But his words, especially concerning the memory of my father, stung me. I gave up the habit.

SENSE OF RESPONSIBILITY

As I grew up, I felt a constant sense of restlessness. I had left school a long time back and there was nothing much to do. Then, gradually, the stories I had heard as a child, tales of great men and women, started trickling back into my mind. A sense of responsibility began to dawn upon me. I would wonder why my home was in such a pathetic condition, unlike the homes of other children who had earning members in their families. I wanted to help my mothers but did not know how. I had no education to get a job, no skills to join a trade and no capital to start a business. But doing nothing was not an option, and I started selling *agarbatti* (incense sticks), and toffees and cotton candy on the pavements of Solapur.

After I had saved some money, I rejoined school and started working in my spare time. While other children had fun, I took up my first formal job at a toffee factory in Solapur for a monthly salary of ten rupees (worth around Rs 14,000 now). The factory owner even gave me a new shirt and a pair of trousers. When I wore the new clothes, I felt a little taller because I was wearing something distinctive after a long time. I would hand over my entire salary to my mothers and receive one rupee as pocket money in return. Buying an ice candy with my own earnings made me feel proud.

My next job was with a printing press at the same salary. Despite bringing in some extra income, making ends meet remained a challenge for the three of us, so hard times persisted. But so did I. A better opportunity came along when Dr Vishnu Ganesh Vaishampayan, a respected physician in Solapur, needed a babysitter for his child. I took up the job on a salary of twelve rupees. Hard work and the eagerness to help others were the two most important values I learnt from the famous doctor.

The doctor was also the patriarch of Solapur's Wadia Hospital, and I would often visit the hospital and double as a ward boy. At the hospital, I met Sonubai Awate, a matron. This turned out to be a decisive bend in my life. I was about twelve or thirteen years old at the time and was looking for more work. So, when she asked me if I could look after children, I said yes and grabbed the opportunity. I was asked to babysit her little daughter for twelve to thirteen rupees a month. From my house, Wadia Hospital was about two kilometres away. So, I used to leave home at 7.30 a.m. and head back from the hospital at around 6.30 p.m. My job was to look after the girl, take her to a missionary school and then bring her back home. I would wait outside her school until the bell rang at the end of the day.

At Sonubai's house, I experienced a cultural ambience I had not known before. People wore different clothes, spoke polished Marathi and treated everyone respectfully. Sonubai was a Muslim from Hyderabad, but the family members were all vegetarians. Although I used to eat mutton and fish at home, the food habits of Sonubai's family influenced me as I discovered new delicacies. Even today, I prefer vegetarian food if there is a choice.

But food was not the only thing that affected me deeply. I was mixing with people whose language, habits and thinking were entirely different from what I had been exposed to until then. I learnt about different cultures. I was exposed to cinema for the first time at their house. I witnessed music functions with them for the first time. I saw Abdul Halim Jaffer Khan, the sitarist, play music and it had a profound impact on me. I developed a taste for music and qawwali. All this is to say that I benefited a lot from staying at their house.

But I was also subjected to shocking treatment. While the family members dined together and ate food served on expensive tableware, I was made to eat out of a cheap metal plate and away from the dining room. I did feel offended by the blatant inequality at their house, but I also realized this treatment was still relatively better than what I had experienced and witnessed in the village. Sonubai's house did not have the same degree of caste discrimination; everyone was friendly.

Outside, it was different. People often assumed that I belonged to an upper caste, perhaps due to my lighter complexion. But the moment they found out, their behaviour around me would change. One time, on my way back home from somewhere, I got very thirsty and asked a man for some water. He asked me about my caste and his demeanour shifted upon hearing my answer. He offered me water in an aluminium utensil, tilting it towards me from an angle so my lips wouldn't touch the container.

While growing up, often, I would not understand the reason for this discrimination. My mother told me to accept the situation but when I went to bed each night, I wept, wondering how people could allow pets everywhere in their house but not a human being. As I continued to work at Sonubai's house, something changed within me. I wanted to overcome the caste barrier through my achievements and chart my own course. This meant struggle would be a constant companion if I wanted to aspire for greater heights in life.

While caste discrimination informs social treatment, education offsets this to some degree. As I moved ahead in life, the discrimination became less stark. In college, for example, I never felt discriminated among friends.

I decided not to harbour any grudges against anyone. Rather than wasting time and energy on negative thinking, I felt that I should make the best use of the situation. This has remained my motto throughout life. I am neither a fatalist nor do I believe in the stars. My conviction is to work hard, excel in my chosen field and, above all, make friends. This attitude would help me later in life. Today, in the twilight of my life, I can say that I am a self-made man and would gladly offer advice to anyone who comes to me for guidance.

If learning about social evils the hard way was a necessary part of my growing up, life also brought me in contact with broad-minded individuals of dominant castes. For instance, there was a Brahmin friend who used to invite me to his house, where we would play, study and eat together. The friend's father knew of my caste but the only forbidden place for me in their house was their *devghar* (puja room). This could be one reason that turned me away forever from idol worship, apart from, of course, shaping my total rejection of the caste structure. Later in life, whenever I would be sworn in before assuming any official position, I would take the oath 'solemnly ...' and not in the name of God. I became a rationalist early in life but never belittled anyone for being a believer. In fact, I would participate in festivals like Ganesh Chaturthi, a hugely popular event in Maharashtra's religious calendar. My fight is against discrimination on account of caste and religion.

Although treated differently at Sonubai's house, I began learning the rules of social etiquette, finesse of language and table manners by observing the others. Pleased with my work, Sonubai offered me a part-time job in the Solapur Ladies' Club. This gave me an opportunity to interact with the upper echelons of society as club membership was restricted to wealthy families and high-ranking government officials. As I listened to their discussions, I came to understand the importance of being successful. Interacting with the rich and famous also gave me confidence, made me aware of my strengths and weaknesses, and ignited a fierce sense of competitiveness within me. My language changed as I heard new words and started using them. My friends in Dhor Gali would often tease me, calling me 'Baman', a corruption of the word Brahmin, but I didn't mind.

I imbibed many new ideas at Sonubai's house, which shaped my personality. For instance, even the disagreements in her house were mild and to the point, with nobody losing their cool. It was there that I acquired the skill to de-escalate conflicts while putting across my point effectively. The atmosphere in her house made me dream about education and school again. I always remembered that my father wanted me to study. I would dress up nicely and go to school, carrying my bag and slate. That life had ended suddenly with his death. But that did not mean I had given up on the dream of going to school again, if—and when—I could afford it.

BACK TO SCHOOL

I used to work at Sonubai's house and get free at 6.30 p.m. On the way back home, there was a night high school run by Vidya Mandir Organization, which started at 7 p.m. Classes were conducted in two or three buildings. One day, I decided to ask them if they would take me in as a student, mentioning that I had only studied until the fifth standard. I went to the headmaster there—R.V. Deshpande—and I explained to him my situation and my financial constraints, while asking for admission. He was a very nice man, but he told me that I was not eligible because there was a gap in my education and that I was older than all the other students there.

But I was determined and would not budge. Sensing my desperation and determination, Deshpande-ji became sympathetic, and said that I should meet the education inspector and tell him my story. Because if he gave me a letter, I was sure to be given admission. So, I—all of thirteen years old—went to the education inspector and told him about my situation, how I couldn't study because of my family's poor financial condition. He agreed to get me admitted to the eighth standard and gave me a letter. Deshpande-ji was very happy to see that I was able to convince the inspector. I think it was my destiny that I was able find this school close to Sonubai's house and resume my education.

During this time, I got involved in dramatics. The school had at least 300 students. The teachers there were appreciative of art, theatre and drama, and would organize regular performances. One of the first roles I played was of a woman called Shanta. I used to go to school every day in the evening and get free around 10 p.m. In ninth standard too, I participated in a play and once again played a female character.

When I look back, I view Deshpande-ji as a godsend in my life. If he had not guided me to go to the education inspector, I would not have gotten this much education. The school admission completely changed my life. I made a strict timetable for myself. Carrying a small lunch box, I would leave home on foot at 7.30 a.m. to reach Wadia Hospital, two-and-a-half miles away. After working in the hospital till 6.30 p.m., I would go to the night school and be there until 10 p.m. By the time I reached home, it would be midnight. After dinner, I would complete my homework by the light of a lantern. My classmates were unaware of my daily grind, but my two mothers were happy when I passed the eighth-standard examination.

When I was studying for SSC, I became very motivated to do well and wanted to join the college. But another opportunity knocked at my door. I saw an advertisement for the job of a boy peon in the Solapur District and Sessions Court, which was close to the night school. When I interviewed for the position, V.N. Palekar, the judge there, said that I needed to get a recommendation letter. I obtained one from an employment officer there and eventually got the appointment. I must say that I met many good people in my life who helped me along the way. This job was a big break for me, as it paid a lot better than the other jobs I had done until then. I was able to contribute substantially to my family's expenses. The new job required me to wear a crisp white uniform, with a red sash and a starched white cap. The uniform gave me a sense of dignity and identity. Even serving tea to the judges would fill my heart with satisfaction. From twelve rupees a month, my salary had increased to seventy rupees, which was like a fortune at the time. My mothers used to give me some amount as pocket money—a practice that continued even after I became a minister.

Years later, after clearing my Secondary School Certificate (SSC) exams, I would be promoted to the post of peon. Six months after that, I would be promoted again—this time to regional section writer with a salary of 120 rupees—a substantial amount and much beyond my expectations. I would buy myself a bicycle and some new clothes. The job of a peon was more like that of a section writer. I was expected to trace the originals of documents, some of them more than a hundred years old. I would navigate the mounds of old files stashed in the record room, always worried about a snake or two catching me unawares. But I digress. I shall return to my experience as a court employee later in this chapter.

For now, I'll go back to the evenings I spent at school, where I would regale my schoolmates by imitating some of the teachers and other staff. The art of mimicry was a talent I had discovered early in life, along with the gift of a sharp memory. I was also fair-skinned, and had clear diction and a good command over language; in short, all the qualities needed to be an actor, an ambition that I had started nursing as I grew up. Shripad Kasegaonkar, our night school teacher, must have noticed my talents, because one evening, after school, he took me aside, and introduced me to the works of various Marathi poets and authors such as Tukaram, Samarth Ramdas, Vishnudas Bhave and Kusumagraj. By the time I had finished reading some of the works, I was hooked. It was as if a new world had opened for me.

One day, Kasegaonkar Sir decided to direct a farcical skit based on the play *Mumbaichi Manase* (*People of Mumbai*) for the school's annual-day function and offered me a role. Because I was fair-skinned and tall, I was chosen to play the role of a woman named Shanta. It was common in those days for men to play women on stage. The character spoke pure Marathi, so I took lessons from Kasegaonkar Sir. The rehearsals would go on till midnight, sometimes even longer, but I never missed one. I learnt how to wear a sari on my own. My experience at the Ladies' Club also came in handy because I had closely observed the mannerisms of high-society ladies who would frequent the club. The role became famous and for a long time, my nickname in the night school was Shanta.

The next character I played was also that of a woman, Gulab, in *Karayla Gelo Ek*. In the last year of night school, I played

Khanderao Ballal, a male character based on Khanderao Ballal, a diplomat and assistant to Rajaram Maharaj as well as Sambhaji Maharaj. There is a story that, once, when Sambhaji Maharaj had gone to war in Goa and his horse started suddenly drowning in a river, Khanderao Ballal bravely got off his own horse and saved the Chhatrapati.

Theatre gave me a sense of liberation. I would often use my leaves and holidays to pursue my passion for it.

Later, in college too, my tryst with theatre continued. In the first year, there was a gathering where a professor had put up a notice for people who were interested in drama. I signed up and was selected to play Dr Kanchan. It was my first time playing a male character during my college years. My performance was so good that I became famous in my college. This helped me get over my fear of socializing with other students, who came from affluent families, unlike me, and I slowly became comfortable around them. But talking to girls was still very nerve-racking. It would take me more time to become close to some of the female students.

Theatre soon became an integral part of my life and I won several prizes for acting, both in Solapur and at state-level competitions across Maharashtra. Through all this, I persisted with my studies while continuing my court job. I was determined to prove that success—especially the realization of one's dreams—was not the prerogative of any single class of people.

Days passed, then months. I continued with this routine of balancing my studies, job and my hobby of acting, which offered me an emotional release from the daily struggle for survival. Soon, it was time for my matriculation examination. But I was in for a disappointment. I had studied hard but failed to clear the exam. Had I discontinued my studies, nobody in my community would have criticized me because I already had a steady job. But I wanted to follow through. I failed my second attempt too, but did not give up. Finally, on my third attempt, I passed the examination with English as one of the subjects, considered a great distinction then. My friends and teachers had tried to dissuade me from opting for English but I was adamant. My hard work and determination had at last paid off. Had I not completed my matriculation and continued in the court job, the highest rank I would have achieved at retirement would have been that of a head peon.

In 1961, I cleared my SSC examination at the age of twenty, several years older than most candidates who appeared for the test that year. But the important thing was that I had passed. Even at that young age, I had realized that ultimately it did not matter how many times one stumbles, but how many times one rises after every failure. I was now determined to study further. I had lost four crucial school years in life's struggles; now, I wanted to graduate while managing my job. Eventually, I became the most qualified person in my community, an achievement even the most optimistic of my well-wishers wouldn't have thought possible for a boy who once hung around sweet shops looking for wrappers tossed away by customers.

My first brush with politics and elections was a disaster. Call it sheer stupidity or bravado, but when contesting for class representative elections, I gave my vote to my opponent in overconfidence and ended up losing the election by just one vote! This was a bolt from the blue and very disappointing. But, as luck would have it, the elected representative was later rusticated and I ended up becoming the class representative. I didn't contest elections in college after that, but I was still very involved in college activities. I used to think sometimes that I was doing too much and should perhaps take it easy, but then I would remind myself I had two mothers and it was my responsibility to look after them. I started saving money as well because I wanted to go to Pune to study law. (My mother, Sakhubai, died on 11 July 1985, having had the pleasure of seeing me function as a state minister. My other mother—whom I never thought of as a 'step' mother—had died a few years before that, on 4 January 1978, after I had become MLA and a full-time politician.) Both of my mothers adored me and meant the world to me. I do not know who said this, but I agree with this quote, 'Life doesn't come with a manual, it comes with a mother.'

I was blessed to have two.

REBELLION AND EYE-OPENER

My life was progressing at an even pace. It was tough but I didn't mind. What irritated me, though, was the constant pressure through my late teenage years to get married. Since I had a steady job, parents of young girls would approach my family with marriage proposals in keeping with the prevailing societal norms. My mother and stepmother too were unhappy that I had not followed the community custom of child marriage.

Another custom dictated that I marry my maternal uncle's daughter but, for the first time, I rebelled and did not budge.

While things were a bit awkward on the home front, life was easier in court, with no such societal pressure. I was just another employee there, doing my job, and faced no discrimination because of my social background. In fact, my colleagues would even share their lunch with me. But just when I had started to forget that I was 'different', reality was driven home the hard way. What happened would be an eye-opener for me.

I had, one day, visited a married cousin in Dhotri, a highly orthodox village ten miles away from Solapur. Having walked all the way under a scorching sun, I had taken a dip in a pond on the way. A little while later, when I was resting in my cousin's house, I heard a commotion outside. The villagers were angry that a Dhor had defiled the well by bathing in it. When I said I didn't believe in casteism, the mob got even more furious; violence appeared inevitable. Finally, wiser counsel prevailed and it was decided to call a priest to purify the well. I emerged physically unscathed, but the experience left a permanent scar on my psyche about the obnoxious caste system.

This was one of the first few times I experienced untouchability and it made me wonder why—if all of us were god's children and followed the same dharma—some of us were branded differently. Birds, animals and insects didn't discriminate among themselves but human beings, distinguished by their highly evolved brains and powers of reasoning, were divided by prejudices and biases that relegated whole communities to the margins of society. That's why Dalits are forced to live in separate settlements outside villages, and I don't think the situation has largely changed even today.

Decades later, when I narrated this incident at a three-day lecture series organized on my life by Sarhad, a Pune-based organization run by Sanjay Nahar, some in the audience shouted, 'Shame, shame'. Students, especially those living in slums, had been specially called to hear the story of a man who had fought against all odds to rise in life. Also seated in the audience were unemployed people and those who had suddenly lost their jobs. The idea behind the lecture series was to inspire those who were struggling with life's challenges not to give up.

My court job lasted eight-and-a-half years. After my first promotion, I became a peon. After matriculation, I was appointed a regional section writer. And, before the end of 1961, I had become a bench clerk, drawing a salary of 150 rupees. I eventually resigned my court job after completing my Bachelor of Arts degree, but I continued to nurture my acting talent and went on to win many trophies for my college. I did not want to stop at becoming an actor; I wanted to be an orator and then a lawyer.

Before I wrap up this chapter, I would like to mention something else that opened my eyes and taught me how important self-respect was. It was common for court peons to ask for money from advocates on occasions like Rang Panchami and Diwali. This practice was called 'asking for a post'. I didn't know what asking for a post meant and, on my first Rang Panchami as a court employee, had accompanied the other peons to the advocates. When one advocate gave a rupee each to the peons and the second advocate also followed suit, I realized it was akin to begging. Horrified, I turned around and walked away.

7

From Genba to Sushilkumar

I ADOPTED THE name Sushilkumar when I was in Sangameshwar College, Solapur. My success in acting and elocution had helped me make many friends in college, and they didn't like my name Genba. They felt that it did not suit me. It was not that I was ashamed of my name, but my friends insisted that I change it. It was a time when I used to dream of landing lead roles as an actor, and making it big in Pune and Mumbai; so I too wanted an attractive name. Film stars like Dilip Kumar, Rajendra Kumar and Raj Kumar, who either chose their stage names or dropped their last names, had all preferred, Kumar, and hence the name was in circulation.

I had even tried my luck in Bollywood, egged on by my friends who would often tell me that with my fair complexion, light-coloured eyes and moustache, I resembled Raj Kapoor. The illusion had ended early after a strapping guard at Mehboob Studio refused to even let me in. Later, when I held the culture and art portfolio as a minister, I would often give the clap for *muhurat* shots for films. One day, I shared with Dilip Kumar my experience with the guard. We both had a good laugh and he later publicized it, saying '*Kabhi darbaan ne inhe roka tha*, *ab ye hamein rokte hai* (Once a guard stopped him, now he stops us).'

Anyway, coming back to what I was saying, I felt a good name was needed for my personal development. I chose this particular name because Sushil Kavalekar, a leading criminal lawyer in Bombay High Court, was a well-known figure in those days. Since I too wanted to become a successful lawyer, I chose Sushilkumar as my new name.

It was in Sangameshwar College that two teachers, S. Bhogishayan and Shriram Pujari, spotted me. Bhogishayan Sir taught us English literature and the way he explained *The Merchant of Venice* is still fresh in my memory. The fatalism portrayed by Shakespeare in the play and the characters created by him left a permanent impression on my young mind. Bhogishayan Sir would explain the finer points in such a manner that the English language became a lifelong passion for me.

Pujari Sir was the doyen of Solapur's cultural life. He took me under his wing, and taught me diction, voice modulation and mastery of the language—qualities necessary to become a successful stage performer. I suppose it was natural for Pujari Sir to spot me. I would go to college wearing ironed trousers and colourful bush shirts with a tie. In fact, from the very first year, I became a hero to my friends and got to act in popular plays like *Prema Tuza Rang Kasa*, *Vegala Vhaychay Mala* and *Lagnachi Bedi*. Acharya Atre was present when *Lagnachi Bedi* was staged. When Atre—a playwright, film producer, editor of the Maratha newspaper and leader of the Samyukta Maharashtra movement—patted my back, I felt I had finally achieved something.

My friends egged me on to contest the election for the post of class representative (CR). After filing my nomination, I got down to canvassing, confident that I would be victorious. Unfortunately, I lost by a single vote. That, however, didn't stop me from becoming CR shortly after. The principal rusticated the elected CR for misbehaving with a girl student and appointed me in his place. This was the first elected office I held and I made the most of it by organizing picnics. I even conducted a socio-economic survey of a few localities in Solapur by enlisting some of my classmates. Such surveys were unheard of in Solapur then.

On the personal front, thanks to my job and the salary I was earning as a court employee, the days of extreme poverty were over. But we were still relatively poor. All my friends were much better off financially and, while I never envied them, I was acutely conscious of my own situation—especially the gap between my financial status and theirs. So I concealed my family's economic condition from my peers and even the fact that I worked as a court peon to maintain myself. From all outward appearances, I came from a sound financial background. It helped that I had already developed a fondness for good clothes and would go to college wearing a tie and sunglasses.

I had constructed my image so meticulously that my fellow students considered me one of them and continued to flock around me, blissfully unaware of my background. Only a few college teachers knew that I was a court peon. I was very careful about keeping up that facade of so-called respectability. One of my responsibilities as a peon was to collect mail for the court. While running such errands, I would wear the court uniform, cycle down to the post office, deposit the mail in court and then return to the college dressed in my usual, stylish attire.

But this carefully preserved façade would crumble soon—sooner than I had expected.

MOMENT OF RECKONING

Solapur court was in the news ahead of a hearing in a sensational case involving Madhav Kazi, a handsome youth, who had duped several girls from wealthy families. Kazi had married seven girls under different names and the newspapers were full of reports about his escapades.

When Kazi was produced in court for the first time, the courtroom was overflowing with spectators, including many girls. I still remember how my announcement—'Madhav Kazi *hazir ho'*—had attracted everyone's attention in the courtroom. In the few seconds it took for Kazi to be brought to the box, all eyes were riveted on me, the court peon in white uniform, red sash and cap. And that was when the image I had carefully built shattered forever. Among the spectators were some students of Sangameshwar College, both boys and girls. When they saw my familiar face beneath the judge's dais, they gasped. I felt like dying on the spot under their piercing gaze—some sneering, some compassionate and some just mesmerized.

I cursed my poverty, which had forced me to take up this court job, and wondered what the girls and the boys who were used to seeing me move around like a hero on the college campus would think of me now. I felt humiliated, thinking that my cover had been blown.

For a moment, I was so ashamed that I wanted to run away from the courtroom. The next moment, I gathered my senses and admonished myself. I was doing an honest job, and there was nothing to be ashamed of. I told myself that the court job was like spending a few minutes in a railway station waiting room. Today, looking back at that episode, I can say that something changed within me that day. In a way, it was I who stood trial in the court of my mind and emerged triumphant. I told myself being poor was not a crime, I overcame my inferiority complex and looked straight back at everybody who stared at me. That was the moment of my triumph over adversity—the first decisive battle of my life that I won.

I resumed life as if nothing had happened and, the next day in college, I asked my friends and classmates if they had attended Kazi's trial the previous day. It was the only way I could hold my head high in a society that pounced on the weak and the less privileged. But whatever apprehensions I had, my fellow students dispelled. They spoke to me normally, in the same way they did before my so-called cover was blown, and nobody ever mentioned my court job. I was back in the mainstream of college life, my perceived unease gone, and, soon, I was working on another of my ambitions—to establish myself as an orator.

One of our teachers, Neelkanth Punde, guided me in the art of public speaking. I had assimilated Marathi classics and my ability to instantly recall things made me a permanent fixture at various inter-college debates. I became the automatic representative of my college and winning prizes in Marathi elocution contests was no longer a novelty. But one weakness haunted me: My feelings of inadequacy in English kept me away from English elocution contests.

I was determined to master the art of oratory in English. My homework extended for longer hours as I started poring over English literature in addition to regular studies. I also aspired to become a judge one day, though I never spoke about this to anyone.

The urge to test my oratorical skills in English made me restless. Then, one day, I finally gathered the courage and registered myself as a contestant. Given my track record in Marathi elocution, my teachers didn't think that I would need any tutoring for the English contest. They forwarded my name, believing that I would bring back one more trophy to our college.

How wrong they were!

ENGLISH ELOCUTION DISASTER

My maiden entry into the arena of English elocution was a fiasco. My earlier stage performances had made me an expert in coming up with impromptu responses and I thought I would try the same technique for English elocution. Unfortunately, it didn't work out that way. Moreover, I was underprepared and the inevitable happened.

The topic for that day was: 'If you want peace, prepare for war'. Mentally, I had constructed a line of argument in Marathi. Then, I had mechanically translated that into English, unaware of the nuances of words and expressions, and how to structure an address in English.

When I stood before the audience, I lost my nerve and didn't know how to start or what to say. With great effort, I came up with what turned out to be my first and last statement of that speech. 'If we want peace, we can go in for cold war,' I mumbled. The audience erupted. I realized I had put my foot in my mouth and there was no point going ahead. Dejected, I left the rostrum and beat a hasty retreat.

But this disaster spurred me on to work harder, and mastering the English language became an obsession. I opted for English not only for extracurricular activities but also for my B.A. examinations. In my final year, I shifted to Dayanand College, a reputable institution, because I wanted to major in political science. In 1965, I topped the list of successful candidates from the college, and was complimented by my peers and teachers.

Although unlettered, my mothers had instinctively understood that, as the first graduate in the family and within my clan, I would like to spread my wings. Solapur had only a couple of degree colleges and, to pursue a career in law, I needed to move to Pune, the nearest and most attractive destination. I resigned from my court job and joined Pune's famed Law College.

Regarded as Maharashtra's cultural and academic capital, Pune had many institutions, each specializing in different branches of knowledge and research. Standing out in such a milieu, I realized, would be possible only for a person of outstanding calibre. Now, nearly six decades later, if anyone were to ask me if I had managed to stand out in Pune's competitive world, I wouldn't be able to come up with a clear answer. But what I can say for sure is that the shift to Pune would prove to be a turning point in my life, in more ways than one.

The first obvious change came in the form of a new involvement. As a law student, I had comparatively little to do once my classes finished by noon. I had been looking for an opportunity to involve myself in student activism and was impressed by Sharad Pawar, who was then at the centre of the student movement in Pune. The atmosphere was charged with nationalist fervour as Pakistan had attacked India and the students were eager to articulate their sentiments. Veteran Congress leader N.V. Gadgil, fondly addressed as Kakasaheb Gadgil, who was the vice-chancellor of Pune University, encouraged the students to take out a procession against the aggression and led the march himself.

ANOTHER TURN

Unknown to me, another turn in my life was already taking shape. Subhash Vilekar, a very close friend of mine, met me one day in Pune. As we got talking, Subhash suddenly brought out a newspaper clipping. It was an advertisement for the post of sub-inspector in Mumbai Police. Then, without giving me any scope to refuse, he filled out an application form and asked me to sign it. I had been prepared for many career options but joining the police was certainly not one of them. I didn't have the heart to say no to Subhash, so I signed the form and forgot all about it. Until the day policeman came looking for me at the college canteen. I was even more stunned when the havaldar saluted me and told me that I had been called for an interview with the 'IGP sahib'.

I decided to go for the interview, telling myself that even if I was rejected, I would at least get a sense of how such interviews are conducted. Having worked in court, I was also not completely unfamiliar with the police department. When I presented myself at the police headquarters, then located in the old secretariat building near Mantralaya, a flicker of hope came alive in my mind as I considered the option seriously. While waiting for my turn, I mentally rehearsed replies to questions I anticipated. This was going to be the second-most important interview of my life, the first being at the Solapur court nine years earlier.

Inspector-General of Police (IGP) S. Majidullah asked me several questions on economics. When he persisted with this line of questioning, I could no longer hold myself back and asked the topmost police officer in the state why he was focusing on economics when I was a student of political science. It was not the most sensible thing to say and I left that day convinced that nothing would come of the interview.

Imagine my surprise when, one day, as I sat with friends in the college canteen, a constable from Deccan Gymkhana, Pune police station came up and saluted me. After identifying himself, he handed over an official khaki envelope. Inside the envelope was the appointment order. I had been told to join the force immediately.

New recruits were required to report to Mumbai for a three-month training course. I was in two minds as I wanted to complete my law degree and return to Solapur to practise in the district court. I was also worried that my dream of becoming a successful lawyer would remain unfulfilled if I joined government service. So, I met vice-chancellor N.V. Gadgil and requested him to allow me to complete my first-year LLB course by attending lectures in Pune every weekend. It took me two attempts to clear the first-year LLB exam, after which I enrolled myself in New Law College in Matunga, Mumbai for the second-year law degree.

After I completed my police training, I was posted as a sub-inspector in the Criminal Investigation Department (CID), considered a dream assignment in the Mumbai police force. I was assigned to the American-European Wing, the most prestigious section, and my job entailed accompanying foreign VVIPs on their visits to Mumbai. Apart from the prestige, I learnt a lot from the conversations I had with foreign visitors on a range of subjects, and my superiors soon found out that I could be sent on any assignment.

Things were at last looking up after those early years of struggle. I brought my mothers to my official quarters in Dadar. With a monthly salary of 350 rupees and a place to stay, my life had settled into a rhythm; though, deep in my heart, I still wanted to become a successful lawyer.

In 1969, I cleared my final LLB examination and became eligible to practise law in Solapur court—taking another step towards fulfilling my dream. It was a proud moment for me, made even more memorable after the mayor of Solapur, Iraian Bolli, felicitated me at a programme held in Dhor Galli. Although I had a steady job with the police, with an assured salary and other benefits, this was what I had wanted. A police officer's job means you are bound to a set of rules and restrictions, but a lawyer has the freedom to study human nature in all its manifestations and help others. The choice seemed like a no-brainer, but, strangely, I was in a dilemma. I couldn't make up my mind.

A local journalist, Vasant Ekbote, who covered the felicitation, came up with what turned out to be a prophetic piece. He wrote that I would neither remain a police officer for long nor continue practising as a lawyer, predicting that I was destined for great social responsibilities.

8
Matters of the Heart

AT THIS JUNCTURE, my life was to take another unexpected turn; this time, in the form of a relationship revived. My friend Subhash Velekar—the one who made me sign the police job form—had two Mumbai-based cousins, Sudhir and Ujwala Vaidya, who were frequent visitors to Solapur.

One day, when Ujwala was in town, I invited her over for a Diwali dinner. Subhash was also there. A few years after that, when I was still studying in Pune and was appointed for a job as a sub-inspector of police in Intelligence in Mumbai (then known as Bombay), I got a job in the foreign squad. My training school was in Dadar and Subhash came to visit me there. Ujwala's house was also in Dadar. He took me to her house for tea. Her brother, Sudhir, was also acquainted with me. Thanks to my expanding social network, my bond with the Vaidya family increased. Hardly a day passed when I did not meet Sudhir and the casual acquaintance soon developed into a close friendship. I became a regular visitor to the Dadar residence of the Vaidya family.

A few years went by like this and our friendship deepened. I sensed that Ujwala liked me, but I was aware that she belonged to an upper caste—the Chandraseniya Kayastha Prabhu (CKP). Ujwala, however, didn't seem to be bothered by such caste-based social differences, her outlook shaped by a cosmopolitan city like Mumbai where she had grown up. Though marriage was certainly on our minds, neither Ujwala nor I brought it up.

And then, suddenly, tragedy struck. Sudhir, who worked at the Cadbury factory, died in a freak road accident. As the grieving Vaidya family retreated into a shell, talking, or even thinking, about marriage became out of the question. Sudhir had also had an inter-caste marriage and he had some idea that I was in love with his sister. After his passing, I didn't know who I could share this with.

While Sudhir's family mourned in silence, I found it difficult to come to terms with the situation. Sudhir had become a close friend and his death affected me deeply. But, apart from this personal loss, his death had an unnerving impact on me. The easy rhythm I had settled into had suddenly been disrupted. Yes, I was popular with my bosses and colleagues; it had become a routine to accompany foreign dignitaries in posh cars to five-star hotels; my salary was comfortable and my mothers were happy. But life still felt incomplete. I wanted a life partner; I wanted to settle down with Ujwala. But this was hardly the time to bring this up.

Another dark thought bothered me. It was true that Ujwala didn't give much importance to caste and other social differences, but the unforeseen tragedy seemed to have cast a shadow on our future relationship. Sudhir had married a woman who was not from his caste and, at the time, the Vaidya household was liberal in its outlook. But Sudhir's untimely death changed that and created a fear that inter-caste marriages were inauspicious. Although no one said anything, I could sense that the family was not too comfortable with the idea of Ujwala and I getting married. I didn't bring up the topic for at least a year after Sudhir's death. Bhaisaheb, the family patriarch, had treated me like his own son and I didn't want to hurt the family's sentiments.

Unaware of my emotional involvement with Ujwala, my mothers and relatives from my wider family kept pestering me to meet some girls they had chosen and select one to be my wife. I had resisted the pressure for so long but, one day, I gave in—finally reconciling myself to life without Ujwala. Soon, a nice-looking girl was chosen, and I was engaged to her. Bizarre as it may sound, Ujwala's parents were also present at my engagement. While I acted as if I was enjoying the post-engagement festivities, I cursed myself for not telling my would-be bride the truth. But then, destiny intervened. My bride was diagnosed with blood cancer and died within two months of our engagement. I decided to remain a bachelor.

CHANCE MEETING

I thought everything was turning against me. It was as if the whole universe had conspired to deny me happiness. In that frame of mind, I felt like I had no right to continue my association with Ujwala. I stopped meeting her and kept away from the Vaidya household. But it was not easy. Much as I tried to forget Ujwala, I couldn't get her off my mind. Day and night I thought about her, but I stuck to my resolve of not making any attempt to meet her, hoping that I would be able to get over the first true love of my life.

Weeks passed. One day, I boarded the double-decker bus number 87 from Worli to Mahim, chose a vacant seat and sat down. As I was lost in my thoughts, I sensed someone sitting next to me. It was Ujwala. We got down at Mahim for a cup of tea. Suddenly, she asked me if I would marry her. After I had regained my composure, I tried to convince her of the futility of meeting again. I told her that I had decided not to get married because every attempt from my side to find love had culminated in tragedy. While I was pouring my heart out, Ujwala looked amused.

'Who will marry an unlucky person like me?' I asked her. 'Will you?'

I thought that would put her off.

Ujwala smiled. 'Yes,' she said. 'I will.'

To test how serious she was, I took her to a jeweller's shop, bought an exquisite *mangal sutra* and proposed to marry her right there.

'When do we marry?' I asked her.

'I leave that to you,' she replied.

I decided that 1st May would be ideal. It was both Labour Day and Maharashtra Day, and we would celebrate our anniversary along with everybody else. Ujwala had no objection to the date, but we both decided not to tell her family for the time being.

We took my family into confidence and only a few friends were to be invited.

On 1 May 1970, a friend of Ujwala's reached the Vaidya home in the morning and took permission from her mother to take her out. The friend's mother later adorned Ujwala in the traditional Maharashtrian wedding attire. My friends, meanwhile, waited at a marriage bureau outside Charni Road suburban railway station. The wedding formalities were over within minutes. We then sent a telegram to the Vaidya family.

The next day, Ujwala and I reached her parents' home with a sense of trepidation. Although upset, Bhaisaheb and Mrs Vaidya welcomed us, even as I sought their forgiveness. All was forgiven, and we were treated to a feast. Once again, I became a member of the Vaidya family—this time, formally.

That then, dear readers, is an account of my early life, the period before my entry into politics. Some of you might find this section too long, which I think it is, but I beg your indulgence. It is a flaw most autobiography writers are susceptible to—such is the unfettered pull of talking about one's own self, though better writers would surely have reined in both their pen and their imagination. Unfortunately, I don't belong to that category.

But I won't waste your time giving excuses because I am impatient to take you through the next few years of my life in the next section—Entry into Politics—which promises to be more interesting.

SECTION IV

Entry into Politics

9

Police to Politics

I HAD STARTED this autobiographical narrative with two of the most important professional assignments of my career—my stints as Union home minister and chief minister of Maharashtra—before going back to my roots, and my years as a hardworking and ambitious young man. But how did I end up as a politician when I had aspired to become a successful lawyer? More surprisingly, how did a junior-level policeman end up as the country's home minister? This section begins with that part of my life—the transition, so to speak—that would draw me into the heart of the intriguing world of politics. Ironically, part of the reason for that transition to politics, and the key political roles it would lead to, was my job as a sub-inspector with Mumbai Police.

In performing my duties as a policeman, I would meet people from different walks of life, many of them politicians or political workers close to politicians. One such person was a Dadar resident named Shriram Lele, who ran a transport business. Lele had been active on labour-related issues and was a member of the inner circle of Sharad Pawar's family. This was a time when Pawar had started looking for promising lieutenants to expand his political network under the supervision of his mentor, Y.B. Chavan.

Outside Maharashtra, the dominant political figure was Indira Gandhi, who had been sweeping one election after another. But Maharashtra was still in the grip of Chavan and the so-called Maratha lobby. Vasantrao Naik, another influential state leader, had completed a decade as chief minister, while Pawar, in his early thirties then, was an up-and-coming young leader who had already established himself as a politician.

I once happened to visit Lele's house, where Pawar used to drop in frequently, and he was there that day too. That was my first meeting with Pawar and, though politics was hardly discussed, I was well aware of who he was. I took a liking to him at that very first meeting. This was, perhaps, the moment political aspirations started stirring within me.

On the other hand, my ambition of donning the black robe and practising in court was becoming stronger, even though I had a secure future in the police department. I was again at a crossroads: While legal practice beckoned, the political arena was opening up. It was a signal that my days in the police department were numbered.

Pawar and I, meanwhile, had developed a close bond. We had started meeting often and both of us were obsessed with the concept of social justice. Then, one day, Pawar suddenly broached the topic. 'Are you ready to contest an Assembly election?' he asked me.

I told him I was thinking of quitting my job as a police officer and starting a legal practice. I would think about his offer some time later. Neither of us pursued the matter and nearly a year passed without any further development.

In the meantime, the political situation in the country was changing like never before. Indira Gandhi was now the all-powerful leader of the nation and had completely sidelined the old guard in the Congress. Chavan had thrown his weight behind her at the time of the party's historic split in 1969. Indira-ji now needed a band of leaders for the Congress Forum for Socialist Action that was being set up in every state.

The forum had been launched by the so-called Young Turks of the party and was led by Chandra Shekhar, a future Prime Minister, and Mohan Dharia, among others. Pawar and Prabhakar Kunte were among its founders in Maharashtra and were looking for young people from challenged backgrounds to join the party. I fitted the bill perfectly and resigned from the police force on 6 November 1971, after Pawar asked me to join the forum. Suryakant Jog, who later became the police chief of Maharashtra, was among those who tried to dissuade me from resigning, asking me why I wanted to join a game of chance like politics when I had a great future in the police force. Many years later, I would be the chief guest at an event held to mark Jog's retirement.

MAIDEN POLITICAL SPEECH

After resigning, I was appointed the convener of the forum on 9 November. It was the most important day of my political career yet, but my entry into actual political work was hardly spectacular. 'Anti-climax' would probably be a better word to describe it. Pawar had asked me to address the forum at a meeting in Pune, where Congress workers were eager to listen to their leader's new 'find'. They were all the more intrigued after local newspapers had splashed the news of a police sub-inspector resigning his job and joining politics.

At the meeting, I took the microphone amidst massive applause—and then promptly, lost my tongue. My speech lasted only a few seconds. All I could mumble from the dais before taking my seat again was 'strengthen the hands of the Prime Minister'. I don't know whether it was the presence of big leaders at the event or lack of practice, but my felicity with words and the ability to captivate the audience deserted me that day.

But that moment would play a decisive role for me—just as my English elocution fiasco had done earlier—as I promised myself that I would spare no effort in mastering the art of public speaking. I had already had enough experience of performing on stage and needed to hone my skills. So I started listening intently to various speakers, observing their body language and their choice of words. I was a film buff and watching movies with a new insight grew into a habit. I studied different actors—how they manifested a variety of emotions and the way they monopolized the screen. I would especially look for scenes where two great thespians confronted each other. Mastering the art of public speaking needed dedication and hard work, and, within a couple of years, I would become an accomplished speaker.

I had great regard for speakers like Chavan and Vasantdada Patil, who could easily explain complicated topics to lay audiences. One lesson I learnt from such towering personalities was not to lose my temper and not to take anyone for granted. Another leader who would leave a permanent imprint on my mind was Madhu Dandavate, a physics professor turned politician, who held portfolios like railways and finance in the Union government, and later became deputy chairman of the Planning Commission, which has since been replaced by the NITI Aayog. Dandavate, who served in the governments of Morarji Desai and V.P. Singh, was always found reading in the Parliament library and was an accomplished speaker.

My entry into politics almost coincided with preparations for the 1972 Maharashtra Assembly elections. Indira Gandhi had returned to power at the Centre with a thumping majority, thanks to the liberation of Bangladesh, while bank nationalization and the abolition of the privy purse were still fresh in people's memory. It was a foregone conclusion that a Congress nomination was a safe ticket to get elected to the legislature.

Chavan and Pawar had been busy examining aspiring candidates for the Assembly elections, and my name came up for consideration when the list for Solapur district was being finalized. Chavan did not know me personally, but when Pawar told him about my background, he agreed to nominate me from Karmala—a constituency reserved for Scheduled Castes. The Maharashtra Pradesh Congress Committee (MPCC) endorsed Chavan's recommendation and forwarded my name, along with others, to Delhi for final clearance.

In those days, the All India Congress Committee hardly ever made changes to lists sent by state units, and my friends presumed that the announcement of my name would be just a formality. I was, therefore, not prepared for the shock when I learnt that the AICC had decided to field Tayappa Hari Sonawane, a former Member of Parliament, to contest from Karmala. Although no reason was given, I later learnt that Babu Jagjivan Ram, an influential central leader, had pushed Sonawane's candidature given his long innings in the party. I was crestfallen but there was no question of challenging the decision of the high command.

10

Dealing with Disappointment

HAVING ALREADY RESIGNED my job, I had little choice but to accept the decision of the central leadership. There was no immediate prospect of being fielded, as the next election was five years away, and the future appeared bleak. By then, Ujwala and I had been blessed with a baby girl, but our financial situation was terrible, with hardly any savings to take care of our family of five, which included my daughter, my wife and my two mothers. Ujwala, however, took everything in her stride, not allowing the disappointment to cast a shadow on our life.

I was dejected but chose not to blame anyone for what had happened and told myself that if one door had closed, another would surely open. I told everyone that it was the beginning of my political career and I should give it sufficient time to take off.

It was in this situation that my dream to practise in court became a reality. I rented a tiny office in Dadar and, soon, my practice began to prosper. In fact, my workload increased so fast that I had to hire a couple of juniors to help me out. In my spare time, I started reading books on social systems, the caste factor and the economy. Like many youths, I too was mesmerized by the appeal of Marxism. During my extensive tours for the Congress Forum, I had minutely observed social conditions and was appalled to see that casteism was still a formidable force to reckon with. I realized that saints like Dnyaneshwar, after whom I had been named, and Basaveshwar, a twelfth-century CE poet-philosopher and social reformer, had been aware of this reality and hence propagated the idea that all humans were equal. Unfortunately, little had changed over the centuries and caste-driven biases were still deeply ingrained in the nation's collective psyche, even decades after Independence. Political freedom had not brought with it deliverance from social issues.

I was upset, but told myself that novices, whether in politics or any other field, didn't have the luxury of forming fixed opinions. Rather, this was the time to watch and learn. That opportunity would arrive when Indira Gandhi visited Solapur. I got to spend time with her and observe her from up close, especially the way she handled a tricky situation. Emboldened by her message, which that I would not like to mention in great detail, I decided to work more forcefully for the Congress ideology. That opportunity too would come sooner than I had expected and propel me into the limelight. The Shankaracharya of Puri, one of the four supreme Hindu pontiffs, had supported the caste system in one of his speeches, and I took up the cudgels on behalf of the Congress Forum and demanded at a public meeting that the seer should be immediately arrested for his statement. Overnight, I became known nationally.

This was also the time when my friends Ramdas Phatate, an income-tax consultant, and Daniel Fernandes, who owned a small factory in Prabhadevi, an upscale Mumbai neighbourhood, became an integral part of my life. After the day's work, we would meet as often as possible. Fernandes would pick me up from my Dadar office in his battered car and the three of us would go on a long drive. Those carefree days worked like an elixir for me. I needed a change of atmosphere and my two friends provided just that. But I kept in touch with Pawar and others in the Congress, though I had temporarily shelved my political ambitions.

Who would have guessed that politics would yank me back so soon? That too right in the middle of the electoral arena.

CHANGE IN POLITICAL FORTUNES

Tayappa Sonawane died in November 1973 and a by-election was declared. At Pawar's insistence, Chavan and the then chief minister of Maharashtra, Vasantrao Naik, forwarded my candidature again to the central leadership. This time, the AICC ratified it.

Given how strong the Congress was then, my success, like that of many other party candidates across Maharashtra, was guaranteed, but I didn't take any chances. After I had filed my nomination, I got down to mobilizing voters, using the car Fernandes had lent for me to use during the campaign. Although chief ministers did not usually campaign in by-elections in those days, Naik made an exception in my case and camped in Karmala for a brief period, and even subtly conveyed to voters that

I would be made a minister if they elected me. Pawar organized funds and the party machinery on my behalf.

I won by a big margin of 20,651 votes, and both my opponents lost their security deposits. In August 1974, two-and-a-half years after I had been denied a ticket for what seemed a mere formality, I entered the hallowed precincts of the Maharashtra Legislative Assembly.

My entry into the Assembly brought no major changes to my routine, except perhaps lengthening my work day. I lived in Andheri by then, and continued my legal practice since I had to support myself financially and often worked till late into the night in my Dadar office. Of course, I was getting a taste of legislative affairs too, but was still on the sidelines, being a newcomer to this aspect of politics. So I also started studying the rules and procedures of the Assembly, and read up on the important rulings by the chair (speaker).

FIRST MINISTERIAL ASSIGNMENT

I had almost forgotten the subtle promise Chief Minister Naik had made to the voters of Karmala, but he kept his word. It was around 11 p.m. on 7 September 1974. I had wrapped up my work for the day and Fernandes had dropped me at my Andheri residence. As soon as I entered, my mother told me that Pawar and Vasantrao Naik had been calling me repeatedly. 'I don't know for what,' she added.

I was surprised. For a moment, I hesitated—it was past midnight—then picked up the receiver and dialled 'Varsha', the chief minister's official residence. His personal assistant (PA) passed on a cryptic message. The chief minister, the PA said, wanted me to come over the next day.

Those steeped in politics would have immediately understood the message, but it was lost on a novice MLA like me. I called on Naik the next day and was told to get ready for my swearing-in. I was to become a minister of state in his government.

A new vista of power and influence was about to open up before me—someone who had once lived a rough life as a fatherless school dropout turned street urchin. I told myself this was possible only because of the democratic process followed by the Congress party, and silently thanked leaders like Chavan, Pawar and Naik, who had given me the opportunity to be a part of this exclusive platform. I was initially hesitant to take up the challenge, having seen the Assembly proceedings where political giants took on each other, but seniors like Pawar and Prabhakar Kunte convinced me.

As minister of state, I was given charge of social welfare, cultural affairs and youth activities—not too bad a beginning for a thirty-three-year-old novice legislator. Destiny had been kind to me and had pulled me back from the brink, but, even in my moment of euphoria, I didn't forget the inequity all around. So, when I entered Mantralaya, the administrative headquarters of the Maharashtra government, the first promise I made to myself was to serve the less privileged and those in distress, because I had seen poverty from very close, and had experienced social ostracism, caste barriers and backwardness in every sense of the term.

11
The Emergency

NAIK WAS REMOVED as chief minister in February 1975 and replaced by the stern disciplinarian, S.B. Chavan. Contrary to speculation that those close to Y.B. Chavan would be dropped from the ministry, Pawar and I both found berths in the new team. Then, on the night of 25 June, just before midnight, Prime Minister Indira Gandhi declared a state of internal Emergency across the country.

After the Emergency was declared, Indira Gandhi's opponents, both within and outside the party, decided to lie low. Chief Minister S.B. Chavan asked me to call on Indira Gandhi in New Delhi. As advised by her, I extensively toured Maharashtra to propagate her twenty-point socio-economic programme for the upliftment of the poor. I accompanied Pawar on many of his tours to interior areas and saw first-hand the condition in which millions of Indians lived. During one such tour, I came up with a novel initiative to rehabilitate beggars while strongly advocating that they should be made self-reliant. I not only announced the plan but also implemented it vigorously.

The Emergency-era restrictions on newspapers to not publish anything against the government proved to be an unintended boon for me as my tours started receiving extensive media coverage. One such tour was to flood-swamped Pandharpur, in south Maharashtra. River Chandrabhaga was in spate and the pilgrim town had turned into an island, encircled by water. I decided to visit the marooned town, disregarding the danger involved in crossing the surging waters. I was young and the spirit of adventure drove me to take the risk. The boat procured for me got entangled in submerged telephone cables and was on the verge of capsizing when another boat came alongside and rescued me. Newspapers flashed the incident on their front pages.

Another incident that caught the media's attention was my act of bailing out a young Harijan (now called Dalit) artiste in Karmala taluka when I was touring the state to promote Indira Gandhi's twenty-point programme. Murlidhar Mang was so poor that he had pledged his harmonium and veena to borrow money, and was now unable to retrieve them from the moneylender. I wrote off his debt and restored the instruments to him. Another time, while travelling to Mumbai from Pune, I saw a boy lying unconscious after being hit by a truck. I stopped and took the boy to a hospital in my ministerial car.

There was no ulterior political design behind these humanitarian acts but, whatever the reason, my popularity was on the rise—even as the Emergency was taking its toll on the Congress party and the government. People saw me as one of the promising young politicians in Maharashtra and, in 1975, the Congress nominated me as a 'model young leader'.

It was during the Emergency that I visited the Pavnar ashram of Acharya Vinoba Bhave. I had long wanted to see the man Mahatma Gandhi had chosen as the first *satyagrahi* decades ago. I was eager to meet him, so I reached fifteen minutes before the scheduled appointment. We began a written exchange because the acharya was under a vow of silence. In a cryptic message, he said, 'One who reaches before time always goes ahead.'

FORTHRIGHT STAND ON RESERVATION

While social welfare was one of my portfolios, I had my own views on reservation. In my speeches, I would always ask the backward castes to reject the crutches of reservation and made a similar appeal in the legislative council too, when there was a demand to include certain sub-castes in the list for the reserved category.

Addressing a gathering of backward-caste party workers in Pune, I told the delegates to first develop themselves and stop hating the upper castes. A speech I delivered in Mumbai turned out to be sensational. I told young people not to stand at the door of the government for some pittance of a dole but to work hard. I said the government would support them, but they should learn to become independent, and rise above untouchability and casteism. I was complimented by the media and several academics for my forthright stand, and was hailed as a harbinger of a new culture.

Another initiative that I would count as successful was the backing I ensured for Tamasha, an old Maharashtrian folk art form that provided wholesome entertainment to the rural masses.

The art form had for long been identified with the lower strata of society and I had seen how talented Tamasha artistes suffered privations. I decided to uplift the entire activity by organizing the 14th State Tamasha Parishad in Solapur in 1976 and declaring that the art form would receive government backing. Eventually, even five-star hotels started inviting Tamasha troupes to perform. The art form would also play a role in government initiatives as I employed Tamasha artistes to popularize the concept of family planning.

Soon, I became the bridge between the world of the arts and the government. The two had developed a love-hate relationship over the years. Some sections of artistes had even started treating the government as an enemy. I wanted to change that mindset and began to systematically cultivate the leading lights in the world of arts.

MINISTER OF STATE (THIRD TIME)

After the 1977 Lok Sabha elections, which saw the Indira Gandhi-led Congress lose power to the Janata alliance, politics in India underwent a sea change. Maharashtra was not impervious to the political storm raging in the country. Y.B. Chavan decided to align with the anti-Indira faction in the Congress. Chief Minister S.B. Chavan had to resign as a sequel to the Emergency, and Vasantdada Patil succeeded him. I was made a minister of state. Entrusted with the public health portfolio, I championed the cause of medical colleges in the state.

Indira-ji floated her own party, the Congress(I), but all prominent leaders had thrown in their lot with Y.B. Chavan, who belonged to the faction opposed to her. When the Assembly elections were announced in 1978, the Congress appeared vulnerable for the first time in Maharashtra, its traditional bastion. The Congress(R) emerged as the second-largest party with sixty-nine seats, and Congress(I) won sixty-two seats. Though many bigwigs bit the dust, I was elected by a margin of more than 11,000 votes from the Solapur-North reserved constituency.

The two Congress parties were not ready to see eye to eye, but their failure to form a government would have seen the Janata Party in power. Eventually, Y.B. Chavan permitted the formation of the first coalition government in Maharashtra with Vasantdada Patil as chief minister and Nashikrao Tirpude as deputy chief minister. The coalition had become unstable because Congress(I) head N.K. Tirpude targeted Chavan and Pawar. I was reluctant to join the coalition but bowed to the party's dictates. Although I continued to follow Chavan and Pawar, I led a public demonstration in Solapur to protest Indira-ji's arrest (on various Emergency-related charges). Slowly, but surely, I was being sucked into the unfolding political turmoil.

MENTOR'S REBELLION

When the monsoon session of the Assembly began in July 1978, Chief Minister Patil was unaware that Pawar had decided to walk out of the government with his supporters. Pawar's sudden resignation from the cabinet on 12 July lit Maharashtra's political fuse. However, the expected crisis appeared to have been averted by the Congress(R)'s CWC's terse command on 16 July that Pawar was not to have any truck with the Janata Party or the Congress(I). The CWC under Y.B. Chavan, who was acting president of the committee in Swaran Singh's absence, saw him playing a crafty game. On the one hand, he was constrained by his loyalty to the CWC to abide by its majority opinion and, on the other, he had to ensure the political solvency of his protégé, i.e., Sharad Pawar, whom he had been grooming for precisely this job.

I was told on the night of 17 July that I would have to resign the next day with some others. Backed by the Janata Party, and some other smaller outfits like the Peasants and Workers Party of India, Pawar managed to cobble together a majority in the lower house of the Assembly. Maharashtra saw the genesis of yet another coalition—the Progressive Democratic Front (PDF); a motley collection of Pawar's breakaway group of forty Congressmen (called the Maharashtra Progressive Congress Legislature Party), the Janata Party, Peasants and Workers Party of India (PWP), Republican Party of India (RPI), Communist Party of India (CPI) and some independents with a collective strength of 180 in the 288-seat Assembly.

I became a cabinet minister in the Progressive Democratic Front (PDF) coalition government and a close confidant of Pawar, who was now the chief minister. My proximity to the chief minister allowed me to see first-hand how the institution called the government functioned and it allowed me to learn many valuable lessons of coalition politics. I must add that while I was a minister in the PDF government of Sharad Pawar, Indira Gandhi's portraits hung on the walls in my home and office. This drew lot of flak from various quarters. People could not understand how a PDF minister was putting Indira-ji's portraits in his house and office. But I remained unfazed and these portraits continued to hang in my office till the Maharashtra Assembly got dissolved. There was a buzz in the media that I would often discuss with Indira-ji political developments in Maharashtra, but I was not that big a leader. Sharad Pawar, who was my chief minister then, did not ask me to remove Indira-ji's portraits. Perhaps he understood the equation I had with Indira-ji. I was indeed fortunate to have had a very good equation with Rajiv-ji too. In fact, I still miss his presence. Had he lived on, India would have been different, more developed and socially far more cohesive.

12

An Indira Loyalist and a Loyal Friend

THE POLITICAL LANDSCAPE would change soon. Within a year and a half, in January 1980, Indira-ji had staged a spectacular comeback at the Centre. Back in the saddle, she promptly dismissed the PDF government, bringing Maharashtra under its first spell of President's Rule.

My joining the Indira Gandhi camp had a somewhat bitter backdrop. A weekly publication in its gossip column had reported that Pawar had made some uncharitable remarks about me. I felt hurt but did not attempt to verify if Pawar had indeed made the remarks. I was already in a dilemma as the Congress led by Indira Gandhi had been given a handsome mandate by the public and I believed that keeping away would go against the popular wish. I discussed the matter in a roundabout way with both Y.B. Chavan and Pawar, and realized that neither was ready to subscribe to my line of thinking. Chavan said he would not come in the way of those who wished to return to the Congress. I was at war with myself. Finally, I made up my mind to join the Congress, but the clash between loyalty and friendship was not over yet. It was decided that I should call on Indira-ji to broach the subject of Pawar and others rejoining the party, but the plan got leaked to the media and was then scrapped.

Eventually, I did call on Indira-ji and discussed the matter thoroughly with her but not before meeting Congress general secretary A.R. Antulay, and leaders like Sanjay Gandhi and Buta Singh. After returning to Mumbai, I briefed Pawar and other leaders on what had transpired. The Prime Minister was firm that Pawar should first rejoin the party and only then could he continue as chief minister. It was clear to all of us that Pawar himself would have to meet her. Indira-ji reiterated to Pawar what I had already conveyed to him, but he was not ready to rejoin the Congress. At least, not yet.

DECISIVE MOMENT

After Pawar's refusal to rejoin, I faced a decisive moment in my political career. A meeting had been called at the Sahyadri State Guest House in Mumbai on 11 February to gauge the mood of PDF constituents and workers. While 136 delegates had been invited from across the state, the venue overflowed with ordinary workers. The mood was evidently against rejoining. I told the workers that the party should merge with Indira-ji's Congress but added that I would go with what the majority decided.

Six days later, on 17 February, the Centre dismissed the PDF government. I tried to reason with myself once again but finally chose to return to the Congress led by Indira Gandhi.

It meant parting ways with Pawar, the man who brought me into politics. I knew that Y.B. Chavan too would feel let down. After considerable anguish, I decided that it was loyalty to the Congress that should take precedence over everything else, even if I found myself isolated in Maharashtra politics. I called on the Prime Minister and informed her of my decision. 'Join now,' she commanded, and I became an Indira Congressman again.

After many years, Chavan would admit that my decision had been correct and timely. Eventually, Chavan too would return, while Pawar would follow suit in 1986.

Although I was back in the Congress, it had become difficult for me to get a ticket from Solapur-North constituency in the summer Assembly elections declared after President's Rule had been lifted. Vested interests were working against me and I felt humiliated when there was a long delay in finalizing my candidature. At one point, I was so disgusted with certain scheming elements that I started thinking of giving up politics and returning to my legal practice. My well-wishers—and there were many—ensured that injustice was not done to me. I won by a margin of over 14,000 votes. This was when Congress candidates were losing all over western Maharashtra, the stronghold of Pawar and Y.B. Chavan. My enemies would, however, succeed in keeping me out of new chief minister A.R. Antulay's cabinet.

I did not hold any ministerial posts between June 1980 and early 1983. But that did not stop me from trying to improve the lot of artistes who had fallen on hard times. My efforts also led to a scheme to help ageing artistes. Apart from that, I continued my legal practice, though half-heartedly; spent time with family and friends; and occasionally wondered if I was frittering away my time and energy on an unproductive activity called politics.

DETERIORATING POLITICS

A.R. Antulay's tenure as chief minister wasn't particularly remarkable, while his successor, Babasaheb Bhosale, angered many with his style of functioning. Bhosale expanded his team to quell the discontent but left me out. Disgruntled MLAs then gathered under my leadership and asked the high command to dismiss Bhosale. I had also moved a privilege motion against Bhosale in the Assembly. The matter finally reached Rajiv Gandhi, who was then the most powerful general secretary of the ruling party.

When I met him, the Prime Minister's elder son snapped at me, '*Aapne kya kar rakha hai* (What have you done)?' He was referring to the privilege motion.

I told him the privilege motion was the last resort as Bhosale's acerbic behaviour had left disciplined workers like me with no other option. I also told him the party was becoming a laughing stock because of Bhosale's quirky behaviour.

Bhosale was removed and replaced with Vasantdada Patil. I wasn't expecting a ministerial berth, given what had happened in the past, but Patil not only made me a minister, he also put me in charge of important portfolios like finance and planning. I had no background or training in financial matters and tried to suggest a few names to escape the responsibility—but to no avail.

A young Sushilkumar Shinde

In his early years in politics, with Smt. Indira Gandhi

With Atal Behari Vajpayee

With Dr Manmohan Singh

Inspecting the Guard of Honour as Governor of Andhra Pradesh

President A.P.J. Abdul Kalam administering the oath of office as Cabinet minster to Sushilkumar Shinde

With BSF jawans

With Sonia Gandhi

On a visit to Canada, at Niagara Falls

Beneath the Christ the Redeemer statue in Rio de Janeiro, Brazil

With US President Barack Obama

With President Pranab Mukherjee

With His Holiness the Dalai Lama

With Rahul Gandhi during the Bharat Jodo Yatra

At a Ganesh puja with his family

After voting in an election with his family

I was partly to blame too for Patil's decision to hand me finance. Earlier, when the chief minister had asked me if I had any preference, I had said I was ready for any portfolio except social justice. It had become a convention in Maharashtra to put a Dalit in charge of the social justice department, but I wasn't keen on that.

As far as Indira Gandhi was concerned, she had wanted to make me the chief minister but the strong sugar lobby did not let that happen. Patil, on his part, held a grudge against Pawar because the latter had unseated him in the past—but he was not against me. Patil told me he never considered me an opponent because whatever I did in the past (backing Pawar) was because of my friendship with him.

MEETING WITH INDIRA GANDHI

After I had taken over as the finance minister of Maharashtra, I got a communication asking me to meet Indira Gandhi. A cooperative yarn unit I had backed in Solapur needed clearance from the central government. I was surprised that the Prime Minister had summoned me when the matter could have easily been handled at a much lower level. Union Minister Pranab Mukherjee was with the PM when I met Indira-ji.

After asking Mukherjee to clear the project, Indira-ji indicated that she would like to meet me in private. After Mukherjee had left, she exchanged pleasantries and steered the conversation towards my friendship with Pawar, a staunch opponent of the Congress then. Everyone knew Pawar was instrumental in bringing me into politics, but I had still chosen to part ways with him. Indira-ji quizzed me in detail about my friendship with him and then suddenly came up with an observation that caught me off guard. 'I am told you never criticize Pawar,' she said.

I knew my political future would depend upon my response. I candidly explained that I owed my political career to him and my friendship with the Maratha leader had remained intact, despite our political differences. On my part, I promised her that I would remember what she said and deal with Pawar in accordance with the Congress policy.

Indira-ji's expression didn't change. I couldn't fathom what was going through her mind but was prepared for the worst. After a pause, she put me at ease, saying that I was a rarity because people often criticized Pawar in front of her, but shook hands with him when they returned to Mumbai.

Vasantdada Patil again became the CM on 1 March 1985, but he resigned less than three months later. In 1985, after Patil resigned, my name did the rounds prominently as a potential successor, but I lost out once again. I was among the few leaders who wanted a sitting legislator to replace Patil. Union Home Minister S.B. Chavan was selected as the leader of the Congress legislature party. Former Chief Minister Shivajirao Nilangekar proposed his name, and I endorsed it. I said at the meeting that I was young and could wait to become chief minister.

STAND ON SAVARKAR

I was presiding over a function held in Nagpur on 25 May 1983, to unveil a statue of Veer Savarkar. I was there because

I held Savarkar in high esteem for his contribution towards the elimination of untouchability and casteism. Balasaheb Deoras, who was then chief of the RSS, was also on the dais. The next day's newspapers carried photographs showing Deoras sitting in a chair and the others on mattresses. A Congress MP remarked that it was high time to question the loyalty of people who choose to sit at the feet of an RSS boss and salute people like Savarkar. I clarified that Deoras had sought our permission to remain seated in a chair because he suffered from diabetes and severe arthritis.

I stood firm in backing Savarkar, arguing that I had great regard for his efforts to end casteism. I belonged to a backward caste, so his efforts had a special significance for me. The matter ended there, but I had made my point.

I wonder often, why, when it comes to Savarkar, we tend to focus so heavily on his ideology of Hindutva? His personality had several other dimensions. Why don't we see the philosopher and scientist in him? In fact, Savarkar often suffered because he strove for social equality and for the uplift of Dalits. Such narrowness of thought is a challenge before us.

I'll conclude this chapter with a note of gratitude to all the Maratha leaders who encouraged me and made it easier for a political novice to not only survive but also thrive in the deceptive and demanding world of politics. Y.B. Chavan, Vasantdada Patil and Sharad Pawar ensured that I was not sidelined. While Pawar introduced me to politics, the political break I needed was given by Vasantrao Naik, who belonged to the backward Banjara community. All these towering leaders gave me the opportunity to work with them. This is the greatness of Maharashtra and its leadership.

Here, I must narrate an incident that I found to be inconsequential at first but have since realized its significance. This was the time Rajiv Gandhi had taken over as Prime Minister after Indira Gandhi's assassination. I was summoned to Delhi. One day, I went to meet Arun Nehru, where former Union Minister and Governor Mohammad Shafi Qureshi was sitting with him. As I was leaving after the courtesy call, Arun Nehru turned to Qureshi to say, '*Yeh* Sushil Shinde *lambi* race *ka ghoda hai. Yeh bahut aage jayega* (This Sushil Shinde will go far).' My friend S.R. Damani, who was MP from Solapur, told me about Arun Nehru's remark. At the time, I had not attached any importance to the remark or to Arun Nehru's acumen, but today, I often wonder what he saw in me that made him say that.

I did not have a lot of conversations with Arun Nehru or, for that matter, other party stalwarts such as Pranab Mukherjee, Arjun Singh, N.D. Tiwari and others. But they were the tallest leaders then, so I used to do courtesy calls with them. Rajiv-ji's personal assistant, Vincent George, and I had a good relationship, which continues to this day. He was totally loyal to Indira Gandhi, Rajiv Gandhi and Sonia Gandhi. He never used to engage in gossip and gave me a lot of political opportunities. Rajiv-ji used to call me sometimes at 2 a.m. in the night, and George was the one who used to facilitate those calls.

I used to meet R.K. Dhawan frequently. One time, N.D. Tiwari and Arjun Singh were waiting, and Dhawan sent me to meet Indira-ji ahead of them.

I contested four elections on General seats—two for the Assembly and two for Lok Sabha. I feel that until you find a place in people's hearts, you cannot win. Even for the General seat, people should feel that the candidate will be a good representative for everyone. When I got elected on the General seat twice, I had six constituencies of rural and urban. Politics used to be quite morals-based at the time and people would vote based on secularism. I lost my footing when Hindutva was on the rise and caste politics started to gain prominence. In that sort of landscape, you cannot win unless are from a particular caste or community. Here, one was BJP politics and the other was Ambedkarite politics. I won more votes against the Ambedkarites, but the Hindutva support was very high. My opponent Sadhu Maharaj was the candidate, and even he hid his caste and produced an SC certificate on which he contested for the Scheduled seat.

I think a candidate has to be popular and capable, and only then can they be elected. When my seat became Reserved in the delimitation process, I lost to BJP because of the Modi wave. Even then, I got a lot of votes. People judge a candidate on the basis on their capability to carry everyone along. I won when I contested on a General ticket but lost the election when I contested on a Reserve-category ticket; I find this fact amusing.

SECTION V

Foreign Visits and Reflections

13

Journey to Geneva

THE YEAR 1979 was a landmark one for me—it marked the first time I travelled outside India. I was to attend a conference in Geneva, one of the several cities I would visit during that trip, soaking in the history and reliving memories of my early excursions into world literature. But wait, I am getting ahead of the story. I owe an explanation to all those who have borne with me so far as to why I have suddenly veered off in the middle of my political narrative to talk about something so different.

Actually, what I am going to talk about in this section is inextricably linked to my career in politics, especially the recognition I received for my ability to solve disputes. That's also the reason I have gone back a few years, from 1983—where we left off in the previous section—to 1979. While chronology lends order to a narrative, a linear account cannot always capture the subtle nuances, life-altering decisions or backstories whose importance to future events is not immediately apparent.

It is one such backstory to which I retrace my steps in this section, before picking up the chronological thread again.

In 1979, I was Maharashtra's labour minister in the Sharad Pawar–led PDF government, which had quite a few trade union leaders in the cabinet. The presence of so many trade union leaders in the cabinet had created a tricky situation as they found it difficult to shed their lifelong association with the movement, which had become synonymous with strikes and labour-related disputes.

Although I had tried my best to end as many disputes as possible through reconciliation between the trade unions and the managements concerned, certain prominent industrial units continued to face labour trouble. Industrialists too had their problems—exacerbated by a distressing cocktail of what they considered unfriendly government policies, and a shortage of power and raw material. At the national level too, the Janata Party government was politically unstable—and not least because of labour leaders. The picture, in short, was rather depressing.

On 8 January 1979, in the late evening, Naval, the third son of Pirojsha Godrej, was brutally stabbed along with his daughter-in-law and mother-in-law, at their Malabar Hills residence. This dastardly attack, incited by a powerful trade union leader in Mumbai, outraged many in the industry and trade circles, and the public at large. After all, the victim was one of those rare industrialists who had forged a personal and emotional bond with his workers. Naval had a reputation for probity and essential goodness, and nobody could believe that he could have enemies. Luckily, though he was stabbed twice in the lower abdomen by the attacker, who was wielding a Rampuri knife, Naval survived.

When I investigated the matter, I was stunned to learn that Naval had been stabbed at the instigation of some trade union leaders. I declared that the government would not remain a silent spectator in the face of such brazen violence and went public, stating that the practice of favouring a particular labour union would be scrapped in view of the seriousness of the situation. Militant labour leader Datta Samant, who led a union in Godrej industries at the time, was later arrested in connection with the assault.

In Pune too, I had tackled many critical situations by bringing all sides to the negotiating table, and the Union government was aware of my interventions. Prime Minister Morarji Desai, himself a Mumbaikar, had been receiving calls from industrialists known to him, requesting that the government step in. One morning, I got a call from the Prime Minister's Office. With some trepidation, I readied to speak to Desai, a former chief minister of what was then known as 'Bombay State'[14] and one of the eldest leaders in the country, fully prepared for a dressing down.

Perhaps the Prime Minister had sensed my anxiety because there was hardly any hint of rebuke in his voice. 'Shinde, how is Bombay?' he asked, as if to break the ice. Even as I was trying to fathom the reason for the call, the PM referred to a multinational

14 Bombay State was a large Indian state created in 1950 from the erstwhile Bombay Presidency, with other regions being added to it in the succeeding years. (Source: 'Bombay State', Wikipedia, as of 30 April 2024, https://en.wikipedia.org/wiki/Bombay_State.)

pharmaceutical company that had been paralysed by labour trouble. The firm produced life-saving drugs and the labour strike had created a crisis. The PM asked me to do something about it and I assured him that I would honour his wish.

Fortunately for me, the strike was led by V.R. Khanolkar, a leader known for his integrity and distaste for violence. I requested Khanolkar to come to the Mantralaya and asked the management to remain present for the meeting as well. The meeting began in a charged atmosphere, with neither side ready to relent. Finally, I produced the ace, and told the two sides that Prime Minister Desai was concerned about the strike and wanted it to end immediately. The strategy worked and, after some haggling, the dispute ended.

I knew the PM retired to bed early, so I decided to convey the news to him the next morning since it was already late. As I was getting ready the next morning, I got a call from the Prime Minister complimenting me on the success of the negotiations. I felt embarrassed and stunned, wondering how a busy person like Desai could remember such a small detail.

A couple of months later, I received a communication from the central government asking me to join the Indian delegation to a conference of the International Labour Organization (ILO) in Geneva. In fact, I was asked to lead the delegation because of my skills in resolving labour disputes. So, that was how I landed in the ancient Swiss city in 1979.

I was permitted to take my wife along on the condition that I pay for her travel and other expenses. Ujwala carried '*achar*' (pickle) and *papad* in great quantities because she did not want to compromise on spicy food. I also got a new suit stitched. Till then, I owned only one suit, which I had first worn in 1964 when my friend Rambabu Gupta got married. He had insisted that I should be attired in a suit as his best man at the wedding. But fifteen years on, this old suit looked a bit worn.

I had about a week at my disposal before we left, and I studied how representatives of various countries would address conferences and emphasize a particular point. I had prepared the structure of my address and it was vetted. I polished it over and over again, and learnt it by heart so that the audience would feel that it was an impromptu speech. When the moment arrived for the Indian delegation to address the ILO meet, I spoke confidently and received a big ovation. I focused on the issue of child labour, especially in the context of India. Despite child labour preventing children from gaining the skills and education needed to get decent work opportunities when they grow up, factors like slow demographic transition, and traditions and cultural expectations, contribute to the persistence of the issue in India. Noting that sustained government efforts had, indeed, led to the decline of child labour in rural areas, I made the argument that the ways to reduce child labour further would include reducing poverty, educating children, raising public awareness, legislation and regulation. The ghost of the college elocution disaster had finally been exorcised!

14

Through a Tourist's Eyes

THE FIRST THING that struck me about Geneva was not the breathtaking view of Lake Geneva but how it rained in Europe. Rainfall in Mumbai is thunderous, deafening and blinding, and often brings the metropolis to a complete halt. In Geneva, the rain appeared to be an integral part of life, gentle and lasting throughout the year. Tourists enjoyed these rains, visited museums and cafes, went on chocolate tours or simply looked for watches. All this against a backdrop of magnificent mountains. The city's salubrious surroundings and the mountains' psychological impact on visitors are perhaps why it has long been a centre for international diplomacy where delegates from different countries gather to thrash out complex disputes. Spectacular views and genuine hospitality—that is how I remember Switzerland. The secret to Swiss beauty lies in the Alps—stunning glacial lakes, fairytale towns and gorgeous castles. It's hard to pinpoint the most scenic places in Switzerland.

My next destination was France, a country whose literature I had fallen in love with as a student. It's difficult to pick favourites from all the works I have read but I'll try and name a few, in no particular order of preference: *Madame Bovary* by Gustave Flaubert, *Candide* by Voltaire, *Dangerous Liaisons* by Pierre Choderlos de Laclos, *Le Père Goriot* by Honoré de Balzac, *The Misanthrope* by Molière, and, among modern works, *The Lover* by Marguerite Duras.

Politically, what impressed me the most during our brief visit to the country was its vibrant democracy. I would agree with Herbert Tuttle, an American historian who, while speaking about French democracy, had remarked, 'The republic can be established if the brain of the country lends itself to the heart in the work.' I am glad that as a democracy and a republic, we too have developed a similar attitude.[15]

On the economic front, France's extensive land area—of which more than half is arable or pastoral land and a quarter is wooded—presents broad opportunities for agriculture and forestry. Rainfall is plentiful throughout most of the country, so water supply is not a problem. Interestingly, the farm sector in France employs relatively few people—about 3 per cent of the labour force—and makes only a small contribution to the GDP, about 2 per cent. Yet, France was then, as it is now, Europe's leading agricultural nation, accounting for more than one-fifth of the total value of output and is alone responsible for more than one-third of the EU's production of oilseeds, cereals and wine.

---

15 Tuttle, Herbert. 'French Democracy', The Atlantic, May 1872, *https://www.theatlantic.com/magazine/archive/1872/05/french-democracy/306915/*.

However, the abiding impression of France that I would come away with was Paris after sundown. While the Eiffel Tower was the first tourist site we visited, it is Paris by night that takes one's breath away as the city comes alive in a splash of lights.

'People travel for the same reason as they collect works of art: Because the best people do it.' That was what Aldous Huxley had said in his book, *Along the Road: Notes & Essays of a Tourist*. I am no one to question Huxley's observation, but Paris to me was a revelation far more fulfilling than any feeling of superiority the writer and philosopher was hinting at.

While travelling through Italy, Venice took me back to Lord Byron's *Ode on Venice*: 'Oh Venice! Venice! when thy marble walls / Are level with the waters, there shall be / A cry of nations o'er thy sunken halls, / A loud lament along the sweeping sea!'

Many poets, thinkers and writers in the nineteenth century feared that the city of Venice, which had endured for over a millennium, would sink under the waters and be lost forever. Thankfully, nothing of that sort has happened yet. The only thing that sank was Shylock the moneylender's chicanery, though literary critics have a more nuanced view on the plot of *The Merchant of Venice.*

I can go on and on about Italy but my observations about Europe would remain incomplete without references to Germany, and, of course, my trips to the United Kingdom, a country I loved visiting again and again.

RELATIONSHIP WITH GERMANY

My visit to Germany was a personal trip. It required a lot of planning and raising of resources. I went as a tourist and a student of contemporary history. Germany had always fascinated me for its sheer grit and determination. While I abhorred the arrogance, racial discrimination and superiority complex of its Nazi period, I admired German resilience and its ability to bounce back. Germany's advances in science, technology, art, culture and literature also left a deep, positive impression.

India was one of the first countries to end the state of war with post-war Germany and among the first to recognize the Federal Republic of Germany (FRG), as the erstwhile West Germany was known then, following the country's division in 1949. The relationship, based on the common values of democracy and rule of law, strengthened significantly in the 1990s—following India's economic liberalization and the end of the Cold War. Here, I will lean upon a note prepared by India's Ministry of External Affairs, documenting how political and economic interaction has increased significantly over the last decades and today, Germany is among India's most important partners, bilaterally as well as in the global context.

Economic and commercial relations between India and Germany date back to the early sixteenth century, when German trading companies from Augsburg and Nuremberg developed a new sea route around Africa, as they sailed in search of precious stones and spices. Thereafter, several German companies were established with the purpose of trading with India and other Asian countries in the sixteenth and eighteenth centuries. Werner von Siemens, founder of the technology conglomerate Siemens, personally supervised the laying of a telegraph line between Kolkata and London, which was completed in 1870. The first wholly owned subsidiary of Bayer in Asia, Farbenfabriken Bayer and Co. Ltd, was set up in Mumbai in 1896.

Indo-German cooperation in trade and technology is one of the most dynamic facets of the bilateral partnership. A joint commission on industrial and economic cooperation is led by the finance minister from the Indian side and the economics minister from the German side. In addition, there are several joint working groups in diverse sectors such as agriculture, automobile, infrastructure, coal, tourism and vocational education. The Indo-German Energy Forum focuses on renewable energy, alternative fuels, energy-efficient technologies and the power sector. The Indo-German Environment Forum focuses on water supply and sanitation, waste management, energy efficiency and the Clean Development Mechanism (CDM) proposed in the Kyoto Protocol.

While India is growing in significance as a trading partner for Germany, there is clearly a great deal of potential still to be realized. Apart from traditional sectors, knowledge-driven sectors hold potential for collaboration in the fields of IT, ITES, biotechnology, auto components, renewable energy, green technology, urban mobility and development, and the entertainment industry. There are several important trade fairs held in Germany, in which Indian companies regularly participate to promote their products and technology. Garments and textile products, chemical products, leather and leather goods, iron, steel and metal goods, electronic components, electrical components, pharmaceutical products and auto components are major items of export from India to Germany. The key German exports to India include electrical generation equipment, auto equipment, complete fabrication plants, bearings, gear equipment, measurement and control equipment, primary chemical products, synthetic material, machine tools, aircraft, and iron and steel sheets.

BACK TO ITALY FOR INTERPOL MEET

I visited Italy once again in November 2012 as Union home minister to address the 81st General Assembly of the International Criminal Police Organization, or Interpol, as it is commonly known. India has been a member since 1949. In my speech at the assembly in Rome, I made a special reference to India's efforts in countering violent extremism and, in particular, terrorism—a global challenge today. By its methods and content, terrorism, I argued, rejects democratic and peaceful means of engagement, and attacks pluralism and multiculturalism as well. Thus, for a liberal, democratic and socially diverse country like India, terrorism and terrorist groups pose a challenge that must be countered and effectively defeated. I reiterated the Indian government's commitment to combating terrorism and extremism in all forms and manifestations as no cause, genuine or imaginary, could justify such violence. I also said that India was committed to bringing to justice the perpetrators of terrorist acts, their masterminds and conspirators, and ensuring their fullest punishment in accordance with the law.

While urging the international community to prioritize the fight against terror, I said there could be no justification for terrorism on any grounds: religious, political, ideological or any other reason. But the fight needs to be comprehensive and sustained, backed by international cooperation to ensure that action is not restricted simply to the perpetrators but also encompasses states that sponsor terror or provide a safe haven to terrorists.

I also took the opportunity to remind the world how the masterminds of one of the most heinous acts of terror in the last century—the 1993 Mumbai bomb blasts, in which 257 people were killed and 713 were injured—were still sitting in safe heavens in Pakistan and yet to be brought to book. Credible intelligence suggests that terrorist outfits are investing in stock markets through spurious companies, setting up fictitious businesses and laundering money. So, it's of utmost importance to detect the sources of such finance, including fake currency, and find ways to staunch the flow of such funds.

In my speech, I dwelt upon the specific dimensions of the fight against terrorism in which Interpol could be of immense value, like links to organized crime, the menace of counterfeit currency and the ability of fugitives to simply evade jurisdictions. Most major terror attacks, successful or aborted, leave their footprints in different countries, but investigative agencies, I said, run into issues of jurisdiction—both international and internal—when they try to collect evidence and connect the dots. This means investigations sometimes don't reach their logical conclusions or get inordinately delayed when they finally do, because of the fuzziness involved in the protocols to be followed in soliciting cooperation.

In fact, the Interpol General Secretariat (IPSG) must play a bigger role in making cooperation easier among law enforcement agencies. I noted this and suggested that Interpol should study the feasibility of putting in place some mechanism for getting informal investigation-related requests, like those for subscriber details and IP addresses, executed as early as possible through companies in possession of such information. I urged the IPSG to help law enforcement agencies of member states build capacity and suggested that the best possible ways of prevention be shared, along with information about training institutes and key resource persons, and that details of investigation, prosecution and other specialized dimensions of enforcement work be collated.

My speech made an impact and was widely appreciated by a number of representatives from Arab, African and Asian nations.

IN THE LAND OF SHAKESPEARE

In the United Kingdom, the first item on my bucket list of private visits was Stratford-upon-Avon. Ever since my professors introduced me to the world of Shakespeare, I had wanted to see the bard's birthplace, hear stories about his family life, and see from up close the Shakespeare Trust's world-class collection of books, manuscripts, pictures and other objects related to the life and times of perhaps the most widely read writer in the English language. I even managed to watch a performance of *The Merchant of Venice* there.

The title page of the first edition of the play, printed in 1600, states that it had been 'divers times acted by the Lord Chamberlain his Servants'. A quick internet search reveals that the first recorded performance of the play was at the court of King James I on Shrove Sunday, 10 February 1605.

When I look back at my long innings since childhood, I often consider my association with books, theatre and poetry a greater treasure than the high offices that destiny bestowed upon me in abundance.

TRIPS TO CHINA AND THE US

My first visit to China was in 1993, at the invitation of the Chinese Communist Party (CCP) and under instructions from the then Prime Minister, P.V. Narasimha Rao, who wanted to strengthen party-to-party relations between the INC and the CCP. The Congress has several such arrangements with leading political parties abroad, such as the African National Congress in South Africa, the Awami League in Bangladesh, the Nepali Congress, the Labour Party in the UK, the Ba'ath Party in Iraq, the Pakistan People's Party, the People's Action Party in Singapore and the Mongolian People's Revolutionary Party. All these parties have regularly been attending AICC sessions along with 'observers' from prominent parties such as the Chinese and Russian communist parties. At AICC plenaries, separate enclosures are earmarked for political representatives from abroad. The Congress has party-to-party fraternal ties with over a dozen political parties abroad.

Our delegation to China also included Ashok Gehlot, D.K. Taradevi, Major Sudhir Sawant, D.D. Lapang and Ram Sewak Chowdhary. The People's Republic of China (PRC) was established on 1 October 1949 and India was the first non-communist country to open an embassy there. On

1 April 1950, India and China established diplomatic relations. Four years later, in 1954, the two countries jointly expounded the Panchsheel Agreement, detailing the Five Principles of Peaceful Coexistence.

As we all know, the Sino-Indian conflict of 1962 led to a serious setback in bilateral ties. India and China restored ambassadorial relations in August 1976, before the then external affairs minister, Atal Bihari Vajpayee's, February 1979 visit revived higher political-level contact between the neighbours. The Chinese foreign minister, Huang Hua, paid a return visit in June 1981.

Seven-and-a-half years later, Prime Minister Rajiv Gandhi visited China in December 1988, when both sides agreed to develop and expand bilateral relations in all fields. They also agreed to establish a joint working group to seek a fair, reasonable and mutually acceptable solution on the boundary question, and also a joint economic group. It was both a landmark and an ice-breaking trip that would play an important role in normalizing relations between the two countries.

As a student, I had always been fascinated by China—an abiding interest stirred no doubt by the Chinese monk Faxian (also referred to as Fa-Hsien and Fa-Hien) who, between 399 and 414 CE, is said to have travelled through Central Asia to India seeking better copies of Buddhist texts than those that were available in China at that time.

The Great Wall of China also had a lot to do with this lasting fascination. So it was hardly surprising that when I stood before a part of this 'absolute masterpiece', which some accounts say is visible from space, I could only stare at the structure spellbound for a few minutes.

Among the other countries I visited was the United States of America, where Rajiv Gandhi had taken me along as a delegate to the United Nations. I was asked to make a speech at the General Assembly in 1985, which was a big thing for me. I spoke on nuclear disarmament—a subject close to Rajiv Gandhi's heart—quoting the Delhi Declaration that read, 'Forty years ago, when atomic bombs were blasted over Hiroshima and Nagasaki, the human race became aware that it could destroy itself, and horror came to dwell among us. Forty years ago, also, the nations of the world gathered to organize the international community, and with the United Nations hope was born for all people ...' As a nation and civilization, we have been an outspoken supporter of nuclear disarmament and non-proliferation. A variety of factors have shaped India's stance, including its historical experiences, strategic interests, international recognition and the Indira-ji-led nuclear test in 1974 that gave us a place at the high table among the nuclear power nations. It was on that trip that I met Sonia Gandhi for the first time, but I'll come back to that later in this book.

IMPRESSED BY ISRAEL

I would like to end this chapter and section with some observations about Israel, a tiny nation with an impressive economic and security environment. Work-related trips have taken me to over thirty countries and, while each trip has been an enriching experience, I can say that we have a lot to learn from Israel, especially things like drip irrigation and other agricultural advancements. In addition to India's robust military cooperation with Israel, we also have a long history of Jewish migration without any persecution of the Jews. From history books, I have learnt how the Maharaja of Cochin had sheltered members of an ancient Jewish settlement when they were marauded by the Portuguese. Many Baghdadi Jews played an important role in Mumbai's rise as a modern metropolis and commercial centre. While on a visit to the country, I also came to know how some Indian Jews have settled in Israel and are great ambassadors for India there.

The moment I landed in Tel Aviv in 1994, along with Shivraj Patil, Vidya Charan Shukla and others, I was struck by the city's cleanliness, discipline and simplicity. Even the Prime Minister's office had only basic furnishing. During my interaction with Israel's then-Prime Minister, Yitzhak Rabin, I kept thinking that this was a man who had made some daring decisions for the sake of peace in the Middle East.

After his historic 1993 handshake with the Palestine Liberation Organization chief, Yasser Arafat, which sealed the Oslo Accords, Rabin had spoken on behalf of the Israeli people. His words still ring in my ears, 'We who have fought against you, the Palestinians, we say to you today, in a loud and clear voice: Enough of blood and tears. Enough!' The accords had resulted in the recognition of Israel by the PLO, and the recognition by

Israel of the PLO as the representative of the Palestinian people and as a partner in bilateral negotiations.[16]

Rabin, Arafat and the former Israel premier Shimon Peres would be jointly awarded the Nobel Peace Prize 1994, for their efforts to create peace in the Middle East. It was a tragedy for the world that a little over two years after his handshake with Arafat, Rabin was assassinated by a fanatic opposed to the signing of the Oslo Accords.

In Israel, I greatly relished Khubz bread, alternatively transliterated as khoubz, khobez, khubez or khubooz. I also visited Jerusalem, the ancient city considered holy to Judaism, Christianity and Islam, the three major Abrahamic religions. Among its 220 historic monuments, the Dome of the Rock stands out: Built in the seventh century CE, it is decorated with geometric and floral motifs, and is recognized by all three religions as the site of Abraham's sacrifice. The Wailing Wall delimits the quarters of the different religious communities, while the Resurrection rotunda in the Church of the Holy Sepulchre houses Christ's tomb. Jerusalem is one place I could visit again and again.

16 'Oslo Accords', Brittanica, as of 30 April 2023, https://www.britannica.com/topic/Oslo-Accords.

SECTION VI

My Years as a Veteran Politician

15

Shift to Delhi

GENEVA TO JERUSALEM. France to China. Rome to New York. The wide world has been my theatre of tangible experience—of realms I had read about only in books. So many countries, so many different types of cultures. What an experience it was! The previous section was all about that—my travels abroad and how enriching they were, emotionally and intellectually. Now, it's time to return home, so to speak, to another experience that would not only be just as fulfilling but also play a crucial role in my development as a politician and public servant: My stint as one of the general secretaries of the All India Congress Committee (AICC). This chapter is about my years in the Congress organization, which also necessarily meant a shift to Delhi.

It was some time after Rajiv Gandhi's assassination in May 1991. Political stability appeared to have returned, and I found no need to visit Delhi. There was also no urgency to rush to the national capital. So naturally, I was surprised to get a call one day from Jitendra Prasada, the powerful AICC secretary to Congress President Narasimha Rao. When I reached Delhi the next day, Prasada told me that Rao, who was also the Prime Minister, wanted me to join national politics. When I met the PM, he asked me to shift to Delhi and work under him. I asked for a day to convey my decision. He seemed amused; it was difficult for him to imagine that someone would need time to think over such an attractive offer. The Prime Minister's face creased into one of his rare smiles when I told him that I must consult my wife and daughters before taking such a decision. Rao saheb, who loved talking to me in chaste Marathi, gave me a seat in the Congress Working Committee, the apex decision-making body of the party. Soon, I was made an AICC general secretary, a post I considered superior to many government posts and positions.

Under Rao saheb, I served as AICC general secretary in charge of Bihar and Madhya Pradesh, and eleven other states, including those in the Northeast. While the assignment was extremely challenging, it taught me the intricacies of democracy and governance—especially in the Northeastern states of India, with their ethnic and linguistic complexities. When I later became a Union minister, my stint as party general secretary and my numerous visits to these states, learning valuable lessons about ground realities in India, would be of great help.

Most leaders from Maharashtra somehow do not feel at home in Delhi. Y.B. Chavan, the tallest leader then among Maharashtra's politicians, was in the national capital for a long time but, till the very end, remained aloof from its political shenanigans. Vasantdada Patil spent some time there as a Congress general secretary under Indira Gandhi, but recounted having felt like a fish out of water. Pawar had been in Delhi for a decade and had a formidable presence; yet, he retained his daily contact with Maharashtra. For me, it was different. When I shifted to Delhi, it wasn't long before I would be immersed in my new assignment.

I was elected to the Rajya Sabha on 4 July 1992 and felt overwhelmed when I stepped inside the Upper House of India's Parliament for the first time. Many illustrious and eminent persons, including Indira Gandhi, Lal Bahadur Shastri, N. Gopalaswami Ayyangar, Govind Ballabh Pant, Y.B. Chavan, M.C. Chagla, Kamlapati Tripathi, Uma Shankar Dixit and Pranab Mukherjee, have been leaders of the Rajya Sabha. The Rajya Sabha had also seen the presence of noted personalities such as Prithviraj Kapoor, Kaka Saheb Kalelkar, Khushwant Singh, Nargis Dutt, Fali Nariman, Kuldip Nayar, Lata Mangeshkar, Sachin Tendulkar, Shabana Azmi and Javed Akhtar. There was a time when I had been immensely inspired by some of them. As I realized that it was the same Dagdu who was now inside the hallowed precincts of the House, I was overcome with emotion. I told myself that I should always take care to not demean the House in any way and take part in debates only after I had done thorough homework.

As my readers would perhaps appreciate, I was an inexperienced young man when I joined politics, with hardly any knowledge of the party organization. But once I became a political full-timer, I quickly learnt how the organization worked; its system of hierarchy—president at the top, followed by vice president, general secretaries, secretaries, organizational secretaries—and their specific duties.

THE CONGRESS FORUM

The organization I had initially joined as a political greenhorn was not a part of the parent body, though it called itself the Congress Forum for Socialist Action. The members of this forum were, however, diehard supporters of the Congress and their love for the party was such that they often acted as a watchdog, pointing out non-implementation of party policies or questioning authoritative attitudes of the party elite towards the rank and file. The forum would also step in to check ideological differences among party leaders. Such pressure groups always strengthen a party and leaders from Nehru-ji to Indira-ji would always appreciate our efforts.

In Maharashtra, the Congress Forum for Socialist Action had Sharad Pawar as president and I was the general secretary. Pawar allowed me to move forward in politics this way. Prabhakar Kunte and Tushar Pawar, both socialist leaders, were among the forum's other leaders. Kunte was the co-founder of the All-India Students Congress (AISC). During the Quit India Movement, as student action was taking shape in Mumbai, he emerged as a leader of the student volunteers. A passionate youth, he inspired the students to create a united, inclusive front. While in his early twenties, Kunte was imprisoned for participating in the movement and kept in the 'Worli Temporary Prison' until 1943, after which he co-founded AISC with Dinkar Sakrikar and Ravindra Varma. During the arrest of the leadership of the 'Bombay Provincial Congress Committee', the AISC took up the task of responding to any redressal of the people like a responsible political party. Kunte's courage was greatly reflected in the AISC's participation in supporting the cause of the Royal Indian Mutiny. As time progressed, he managed to garner influence in the Congress Socialist Party.

As a student leader, he toured Wardha under the inspiration of Congress Socialist Party leaders like Achyut Patwardhan, Nanasaheb Gore and P.S. Sane. His journey in the final days of India's independence movement can be described as that of a student leader who was ready to don the reputation of a mature political leader. Kunte remained an active participant in the scenario that emerged post-Independence. He continued his political activities and later became a minister in the Maharashtra government. His life didn't just inspire his colleagues and volunteers but also moulded persons like me to contribute to India's development after Independence.

It was, therefore, my honour and privilege to have learnt a lot from them about the workings of the Sangathan. At many of the meetings of the forum, people like Mohan Dharia, Chandra Shekhar, and Y.B. Chavan would come and speak to us.

Barrister Vitthalrao Gadgil was also a member of the forum, and I would often take advice from him. He was an ideologue, theoretician and truly a man of letters, who wrote books on judicial administration and law. In addition to serving as a Union minister, Gadgil was also a senior advocate in the Supreme Court, an honorary professor of economics at Ruparel College, Mumbai, and a professor of constitutional law at New Law College, Mumbai. Actress Smita Patil's father, Shivajirao Patil, who was a good parliamentarian, also worked for the forum.

When I joined the forum, I was told that all these leaders worked towards a Leftist ideology within the Congress, which was pro-poor. As a young man, I had always been attracted to Leftist and socialist ideals, and would often quote Lenin to argue that a party's duty was to lead the masses and not merely to reflect the average political level of the masses. I was immediately attracted towards the line of thinking of these Congress leaders.

The forum used to send people from village to village to build a base at the grassroots, and I would often volunteer to go with them. Consequently, party workers across Maharashtra, particularly in the rural areas, started recognizing me as a leader, which also helped in my rise within the Congress.

STAGE FRIGHT IN PUNE

My interaction with the forum in Pune was, however, not very promising to begin with. I still remember that day when my seniors had asked me to speak on a resolution. It was the first such experience for me after I was formally inducted into the party. I went up to the stage and, after expressing my support for the resolution, sat down again without making a structured speech. This was the second instance of stage fright getting the better of me and thankfully the last.

Earlier, as a second-year college student, I had participated in an English extempore speech competition, which I have written about in a previous chapter. It was a disaster. Performance anxiety can affect all kinds of people who have to appear in front of an audience: musicians, dancers, politicians and even athletes.

As for public speaking, I want to say that it is all right to make mistakes; the important thing is not to repeat them.

In that speech at the college event, I had said, 'We don't want war; we want cold war.' What I had intended to suggest was a middle path between war and peace. The audience had burst out laughing and I lost my tongue. One of my professors later explained to me what Cold War meant. After that speech, I read books and articles on the Cold War and international relations. A good speaker needs to study a lot, and engage in debates and discussions with peers. Don't be afraid of making mistakes; you'll falter once or even twice, but you'll learn from your mistakes.

MUSINGS ON IDEOLOGY

In my college days, I had a curious mix of communist, socialist and Gandhian friends. It was after college that I was introduced to other ideologies such as socialism—and how Fabian socialism differed from Marxian socialism—free-market ideology and egalitarianism. But I was most attracted to the philosophy of the Congress and its 'duty' of leading the nation.

Speaking in Jaipur in 1948, Dr Pattabhi Sitaramayya had equated the Congress ideology closely with the Indian nation. He told his colleagues at that meeting:

> The Congress is the service station of the life-giving ideology of the nation. The life-sustaining doctrines are pumped through the arteries of the government of the nation, where they become somewhat sullied in

> implementation and are returned to the Congress for purification. The ideology, constantly discussed by the populace and constantly renovated as public opinion, is once again canalized by the Congress through the government in a renovated form, that is how the Congress and the government act and react upon each other.[17]

Similarly, in 1955, INC President U.N. Dhebar had stated with a poet's flair:

> What is the Congress? It is a tear, fallen from the sufferings and agonized heart of humanity in bondage, coming to life. The tear was destined to become a stream, the stream a river and the river a mighty Ganga or Brahmaputra, which was to wash off its sins and weaknesses of ages, to weld her people together, breathe new life and new spirit into their heart, and carry them afloat, united, purified and strengthened by their cherished goal ...[18]

Now, after my long innings in politics, I feel that there is a need to tweak and reform the party's ideology. The Congress, as we understand, also benefitted from those who had come from socialist ideology such as K.D. Malviya, Acharya Narendra Deva and Indira Gandhi's husband, Feroze Gandhi. That's why,

---

17 Johari, J.C. *Indian National Congress Since Independence* (New Delhi: Lotus Press, 2006), xii.

18 Ibid., xviii.

as Congress persons, we should have a deep and structured understanding of other political ideologies as well. Many would argue that Feroze Gandhi was seldom in ideological agreement with the Congress, yet Pandit Nehru was fond of him. This only showed that Pandit-ji encouraged people of diverse opinions and helped them progress in the public sphere. I feel that this is the outlook that everyone should have to create an environment of mutual co-existence.

Nehru-ji, to my mind, had articulated the bottom line of the Congress's secular creed at a meeting at the Ramlila Ground on Gandhi Jayanti in 1951. 'If any man raises his hand against another in the name of religion, I shall fight him till the last breath of my life, whether from within the government or outside.'

Moreover, I think that the Congress Pradesh Adhyaksh (state party unit chief) is like our leader and they should get attention from us, which they do not. This is because people are more drawn towards political power and offices such as the chief minister. But it is important to realize that you can hold on to power only if the party remains strong internally. We have seen examples of this in many parties in recent times.

Towards the end of Narasimha Rao's tenure in 1996, Bhuvanesh Chaturvedi, who was a minister of state, told me that the PM wanted to make me a minister of state at the Centre and that I should accept it. I felt that accepting this post with only four months remaining in Rao's tenure as PM would not be a wise decision. I was happy to work for the party as AICC general secretary, a post that gave me immense satisfaction as a party worker. When I declined a ministerial assignment, the post was given to Suresh Kalmadi. Had I accepted that role, I may not have got into the Union cabinet in 2004 because the tag of a junior minister is difficult to shed.

A place in the Union cabinet was, however, still quite a few years away. Before that, I would contest the 2002 vice-presidential election for the country's second-highest post in order of precedence, then return to Maharashtra for a brief stint as chief minister. In November 2004, I would move to Andhra Pradesh as governor of the then-undivided state. My vice-presidential bid would, predictably, end in defeat, given the political arithmetic then, but the very fact that my party chose me as its candidate was enough to gladden my heart. The next chapter is about this election.

16

Vice-Presidential Bid

I WAS A member of the Lok Sabha and active in the party when Sonia Gandhi called me one day in July 2002. This was a time when Congress circles were abuzz with malicious stories that Sonia-ji had certain reservations about me. I was, however, blissfully unaware of these rumours. So I was surprised when she called me to say that she had misunderstood me. I shall never forget those words, which conveyed much more than what was said. Sonia-ji was one of the country's most powerful leaders, and I was just an ordinary Congress worker. Yet, she was so candid with me and so gracious.

She asked me to file my nomination for the upcoming vice-presidential election. My first reaction was disbelief. The post of vice president is the second-highest constitutional post after the President and theoretically the first in the line of succession to presidency. Once Sonia-ji's words had sunk in, I also felt an overwhelming sense of fulfilment. More than the opportunity to contest for such a high office, it was her faith in me that was truly moving.

On the ground, however, there was little scope for emotion. Krishan Kant was the outgoing vice president, and there was a lot of politics going on as part of the build-up to the 2002 presidential and vice-presidential elections.

Krishan Kant-ji, a seventy-five-year-old Gandhian and freedom fighter, had emerged as a possible consensus candidate for the presidency after the ruling National Democratic Alliance (NDA) and the Opposition failed to agree on former Maharashtra governor P.C. Alexander or the incumbent President, K.R. Narayanan. At the last minute, the ruling combine decided to field Dr A.P.J. Abdul Kalam instead. The Congress and the Samajwadi Party both endorsed Abdul Kalam's candidature. The BJP and Prime Minister Atal Bihari Vajpayee then proposed Bhairon Singh Shekhawat's name as the NDA's vice-presidential nominee.

Sonia Gandhi had then held discussions on the Opposition's nominee for vice president, with Left leaders Harkishan Singh Surjeet and A.B. Bardhan, Rashtriya Janata Dal boss Lalu Prasad Yadav and Samajwadi Party leader Mulayam Singh Yadav. The response to my nomination from various political parties and leaders was amazing—though it was obvious that I would not win the election because of the political arithmetic.

Sonia-ji held me by the hand when I was taken in a procession to the office of the returning officer. The leaders of all the Opposition parties also made it a point to accompany me. The NCP even proposed my name, though party boss Sharad Pawar and Shekhawat were thick friends.

I remember S. Jaipal Reddy, who was the AICC spokesperson then, saying that three of the four top political offices in the country were being sought to be occupied by hardcore products of the RSS. He said Prime Minister Vajpayee, Deputy Prime Minister L.K. Advani and Shekhawat, who was contesting for the post of vice president, proudly claimed to be RSS products. 'This is not merely communalization of the NDA but of the Indian polity,' Jaipal Reddy said, justifying my candidature. The fourth person was President A.P.J. Kalam. Kalam was considered a 'People's President' as he did not come from a political background.

The Left parties released a joint statement extending their support as well. 'The Left parties have all along maintained that a political contest must take place for the post of the President and Vice-President given the present political context in the country,' the CPI(M), CPI, Revolutionary Socialist Party (RSP) and the Forward Bloc said in their joint statement, adding that Shekhawat was a prominent BJP leader with close links with the RSS.

The Left statement also mentioned a purported comment by Shekhawat, who was the leader of the Opposition in the Rajasthan Assembly then, to make a significant observation: 'If the state government [of Rajasthan led by the Congress] continues with its policy of appeasing a particular community, Rajasthan would face a situation similar to that of Gujarat.'[19]

---

19 'Left Supports Shinde for V. President: Press statement', Communist Party of India (Marxist), 9 August 2009, https://cpim.org/left-supports-shide-v-president/#.

Gujarat, it may be recalled, had only a few months earlier witnessed widespread riots, considered the country's worst since the violent aftermath of the Partition left a trail of devastation. The February–March riots in the state would leave over a thousand people dead and force more than a lakh to flee their homes for the relative safety of relief camps. It was in this context that the Left parties decided that it was imperative to oppose the BJP–NDA nominee and support my candidature.

BANKING ON A KEY QUESTION

At this point, one might ask why I had agreed to fight this election when it was obvious who would win. My reply to that would be this: I entered the contest not by depending on numbers but by banking on a key ideological and political question. *What do you vote for—fundamentalism or secularism?* I was optimistic that the majority of our parliamentarians were secularists and hoped that the numbers game could be overshadowed by conscience. Our Constitution is, after all, based on democratic principles and the path it has directed us to follow is that of secularism.

As it turned out, I had hoped for too much.

The ruling NDA's candidate, Shekhawat, a three-time chief minister of Rajasthan, had a clear edge in the 790-member electoral college consisting of Lok Sabha and Rajya Sabha members. I made every possible effort to consolidate votes and even travelled to Chennai to speak to All India Anna Dravida Munnetra Kazhagam (AIADMK) leader J. Jayalalithaa. But Shekhawat's Rajput lineage stretched across party lines.

If at all there was any caste bonding, it was among the ninety Rajput MPs who backed their fellow Rajput while as many as fifty-five Scheduled Caste and Scheduled Tribe MPs did not vote for me.

The fact that the 155 SC/ST MPs in Parliament did not back me was not surprising as the marginalized sections of society are not particularly known for cohesiveness or shrewd political calculations. Rather, they tend to become tools in the political machination and games that upper-caste protagonists play.

Still, this lack of unity was glaring, because I had been a prominent member of the SC–ST Parliamentary Forum. I would also like to point out that some time in 2001, as many as 126 SC/ST MPs had adopted a resolution that someone representing our communities must be there as a contestant, either in a presidential election or in a vice-presidential election. Thereafter, about sixty MPs had led an all-party Scheduled Caste delegation to Prime Minister Atal Bihari Vajpayee. The BJP's Sangh Priya Gautam was the chairman of the SC–ST Parliamentary Forum. When we met Vajpayee-ji, we had requested him to give either the office of the President or the vice president to someone from our communities. Vajpayee-ji was somewhat evasive in his reply and said the elections were still a long time away. At that point, I had no idea that I would be contesting the vice-presidential polls the following year.

After the voting was over, the result showed that more than forty-five MPs had cross-voted in favour of the NDA candidate, while twenty-two MPs had abstained. Among those who did not vote were nine from the Trinamool Congress, despite last-minute efforts by the NDA to persuade Mamata Banerjee to back Shekhawat. The Prime Minister's emissary, Vijay Goel, had met the Trinamool leader at Jantar Mantar but failed to convince her. Goel had even requested her to speak to the PM, but Banerjee refused. This was when Trinamool was an NDA partner.

Among the others who abstained were Dr Jayanta Rongpi, Simranjit Singh Mann, Maneka Gandhi, Lata Mangeshkar, Narendra Mohan, Pappu Yadav, Ganti Vijaya Kumari (wife of former Lok Sabha Speaker G.M.C. Balayogi), Mrinal Sen, Shabana Azmi and V.M. Sudheeran.

A RECORD, EVEN IN DEFEAT

Eventually, Shekhawat polled 454 out of the 766 votes cast; I got 305 votes. There were 759 valid votes: 7 votes were dubbed as invalid in a turnout of 766, while 24 MPs abstained. But, even in defeat, I set a record. There had been 10 elections for the post of vice president so far, but no defeated candidate had got 300 or more votes.

I am tempted to mention here that according to Clause (1) of Article 66 of the Constitution, as originally enacted, the vice president was to be elected by the members of both Houses of Parliament assembled at a joint meeting, per the system of proportional representation using a single transferable vote. Subsequently, it was felt on closer consideration that the various stages of an important election of this character could not be satisfactorily or conveniently covered at a joint meeting of

700-odd persons assembled at one place. The clause was accordingly amended by the Constitution (Eleventh Amendment) Act, 1961, providing for election 'by the members of an Electoral College consisting of the members of both Houses of Parliament', thereby dispensing with the earlier requirement of a joint meeting of members of both Houses. Had the old original election process held ground, I would have been more fortunate as the system of proportional representation could have gone in my favour.

17
Governor of Andhra Pradesh

IN AN EARLIER chapter, I had mentioned how, in 2004, despite delivering Maharashtra to the Congress-led coalition in the state, I was denied a second stint as chief minister by Sharad Pawar's NCP and a lobby from within my own party. Some of the behind-the-scenes machinations had upset me as I couldn't understand how some people in the Delhi Durbar could work in such a Machiavellian way. What saw me through those difficult hours was Sonia Gandhi's support and faith in me. In the presence of AICC observers Ghulam Nabi Azad and Margaret Alva, she told me that while she was in my favour, the circumstances were such that somebody else would have to be appointed as the chief minister. I accepted her decision.

Sonia-ji also told me that she would ensure that I wasn't entirely denied, to which I replied that I was happy to have her blessings. That very day the decision was finalized and I was asked to take charge as governor of what was then undivided Andhra Pradesh. (The new state of Telangana would be carved out only in 2014, after a decades-long movement for separation.) Again, I accepted the decision without any hesitation. Whatever opinion people might have about my unquestioning loyalty to Sonia-ji and the Congress, I have always believed that every office I occupied during my political career was singularly due to my association with the party and my leadership's faith in my abilities.

Of course, the job of a governor is vastly different from that of a chief minister. It was not an easy transition, especially for someone who had been in the thick of electoral politics and preparing for another stint at the helm of his state. Well, let's put it this way: I took my new assignment as just another job I had to do. And the best way to do that, I felt, was to stick to the basic principles I followed.

As chief minister of Maharashtra, I was accessible to everyone and I continued that practice at the Raj Bhavan in Hyderabad, even appointing a teacher who helped me polish my Telugu—the language spoken in Andhra Pradesh. It's a language I was already familiar with since my childhood in my hometown, Solapur, whose southern part is near Karnataka and present-day Telangana. When the staff at the Raj Bhavan explained to me the leisurely schedule of a governor, I told them it would be tough passing my time because I was used to working eighteen hours a day. Maybe, I said, I would learn painting to keep myself busy.

Jokes apart, I did change many practices at the Raj Bhavan.

At the Raj Bhavan, you are required to meet only a limited number of people, but I made it a point to meet as many people as I could and toured every district during my tenure. So, as time passed, people felt confident about approaching me with their problems. It helped that the chief minister of Andhra Pradesh at that time, Y.S. Rajasekhara Reddy, was also from the Congress and junior to me, which meant there was no objection from that end.

I also issued specific instructions that I would love to see my grandchildren mingling with the children of Class IV staff. During Diwali, I invited my grandchildren and other family members to celebrate the festival with me in Hyderabad. It was such a delight to see my grandchildren playing, intermingling and joining in festivities with the Class IV employees and their families. Some said that they had witnessed such a get-together for the first time in their lives. When Prime Minister Manmohan Singh came two days after Diwali, he distributed sweets to the children living inside the Raj Bhavan. The Special Protection Group (SPG), which looks after the security of the Prime Minister, wanted the children to queue up but I intervened, requesting the PM to meet and greet every child on the Raj Bhavan lawn. Dr Manmohan Singh readily agreed and enjoyed the interaction with the children. He then asked the Raj Bhavan staff and their wives to join for high tea.

As governor, I adopted a new way to improve and nurture the relationship with the chief minister. While our Constitution requires that the CM and governor complement and support each other, what we see these days is a lot of conflict between the two, which is unfortunate. So, when I returned from tours, I would brief Rajasekhara Reddy, who was a dynamic face of the party, on areas that needed improvement. He appreciated these efforts, and we established a good relationship.

When I was about to complete six months as governor, I came up with the idea of calling on the President of India to inform him about my observations. I prepared a report and presented it to the President at a meeting that lasted thirty-five minutes.

A HINT FROM THE PM

In November 2004, shortly after I had assumed charge as governor, Prime Minister Manmohan Singh visited Hyderabad to launch the National Food-for-Work Programme. He was new to his job too, having taken over as Prime Minister only six months earlier. While staying at the Raj Bhavan, he told the media during an interaction that his government had done 'reasonably well' so far, despite the hurdles the Opposition had placed in its way in the initial days.

Before leaving for Delhi, the Prime Minister told me, in a voice no one else could hear, that he would like to have me in his council of ministers. I grinned, acknowledging his affection for me. Little did I know then that in less than fifteen months, I would join the Union cabinet as power minister. But more about that in the next chapter.

ROLE OF GOVERNOR

I feel that the office of the governor should never be politicized. Unfortunately, that is very much the trend now, and I think it is harmful to our polity. The only solution for this is that all governors should try and stick to what the Constitution says, and maintain their freedom from party influences as the Constitution expects them to. It is worth recalling here what the Sarkaria Commission had said about the office and the role of governors in its recommendations after Indira Gandhi had appointed the panel in 1983 to look into Centre-state relations. The commission had said that a governor should be a respected individual, an outsider to the state concerned, impartial and not overly involved in the state's regional politics. Keeping this in mind, during my nearly fifteen-month stint at Hyderabad's Raj Bhavan, I never made a political statement.

At the Raj Bhavan, I would often spend long hours on contemplation, practising what Aristotle had said, 'The ultimate value of life depends upon awareness and the power of contemplation rather than upon mere survival.'

I try to be happy in every situation. I have experienced many ups and downs in my long life of eighty-plus years, including prolonged periods of utter helplessness, but I have also enjoyed such moments of pleasure that they seemed as if I were living a dream. A court peon to a lawyer, an aspiring actor to a popular speaker, a police sub-inspector to a minister, an ordinary Congress worker to a party general secretary—that has been my life.

I am happy because I have always had friends who loved me, whether in college or later, and peers who encouraged me, while my marital life has been one of deep satisfaction. But I have not forgotten the privations of those early years when food was a luxury, homework was an overtime activity that often stretched late into the night and menial work was the order of the day.

Just to relive those memories, I occasionally eat the food that used to be my staple diet during those difficult years: roti with chutney. One should never forget their past while enjoying the pleasures of the present. In a way, that difficult period of my life is my guru, because it taught me to face any situation with a smile.

18

Union Minister for Power

IT WAS 30 January 2006. My tenure at the Raj Bhavan in Hyderabad had just ended, but a new innings had already begun—this time in the Union cabinet as minister for power. So there I was, a member of Dr Manmohan Singh's council of ministers—as the Prime Minister had wanted—shifted from the leisurely ambience of a Raj Bhavan, and into the throbbing heart of projects and decision-making at the Centre. It would be my first experience in the Central government and also my longest stint in any ministerial role.

When I took over as power minister, the problems and inadequacies the sector faced were many. The challenges included last-mile connectivity; demand build-up measures; unequal distribution; erratic pricing; overrated capacity; lack of adequate coal supply; transmission-, distribution- and consumer-level losses; resistance to energy efficiency in the residential building sector; resistance to nuclear energy; power theft; and poor gas pipeline connectivity and infrastructure. How I tackled these tricky issues would require a whole volume on each. All I can say here, with a degree of satisfaction, is that the present is reaping the fruits of my labour, and the dedication and determination of my team.

Now, looking back at my six-and-a-half-year run at the power ministry, I have this to say: Each state should generate electricity of its own. Power is on the Concurrent List and it is my considered opinion that the states must build their capacity in power generation, while the Central government supplements that.

But before I go into the details of my tenure as power minister, a quick statistical recap.

By 2010, we, as a country, had been generating about 2 lakh megawatts of electricity. On average, power generation had increased by 20,500 MW under my watch. For the coordinated development of the hydroelectricity sector, I launched an initiative to generate 50,000 MW of hydel power. Additionally, I identified sites for generating thermal capacity of over 100,000 MW and implemented Ultra Mega Power projects of 4,000 MW each to achieve the benefit of economy of sale and procurement of hydroelectric power from Bhutan. Finally, I launched the Rajiv Gandhi Grameen Vidyutikaran Yojana (RGGVY), a part of our Bharat Nirman project to develop rural infrastructure at an initial project cost of Rs 1.76 trillion. Its first aim was to provide electricity connections to 23 million poor households in 1,18,000 villages.

Electricity, as we understand, is crucial for everyone, because it can also mean an increase in income. A villager in Odisha, for instance, would want electricity so that she can use a fan to separate husk from rice, which would improve her household's agricultural productivity.

The electricity sector in India has evolved significantly to provide a wide range of opportunities across the value chain, for both regulated and deregulated businesses. India's power market is the world's fifth largest in terms of generation capacity and the third largest in terms of network. Increasing demand, network extension and upgrade, reduction in energy intensity, unbundling of supply services, and growth of cross-border trade present various opportunities for this industry.

When I moved from the power ministry to the home ministry on 31 July 2012, I recall that the *Business World* magazine had described me as a person who managed to literally emerge from the darkness of India and land in North Block. However, several challenges remain. These include fuel supply, counter-party risk posed by distribution companies, monopoly restrictions on open access and the availability of project finance.

ONE NATION, ONE GRID, ONE FREQUENCY

One of my key achievements as power minister was the big stride the sector would take towards the successful completion of the 'One Nation-One Grid-One Frequency' plan. The synchronization of all the regional grids would go a long way towards optimal utilization of scarce natural resources through the transfer of power from resource-centric regions to load-centric regions. Moreover, it paved the way for the establishment of a vibrant electricity market that facilitated the trade of power across regions.

National grid management on a regional basis had been started in the sixties and, for planning and operational purposes, it was divided into five regional grids—northern, eastern, western, north-eastern and southern. Subsequently, the integration of regional grids was conceptualized. In August 2006, the northern and eastern grids were interconnected. After that four regional grids were synchronously connected, forming a Central Grid operating at one frequency. By December 2013, the southern region had been connected to the Central Grid, thereby achieving the objective of 'One Nation-One Grid-One Frequency' synchronization.

Another aspect we focused on was ensuring that the grid frequency always remained within the 49.90–50.05 Hz (hertz) band. Maintaining a consistent electrical frequency is important because multiple frequencies cannot operate alongside each other without damaging equipment. This has serious implications when providing electricity on a national scale.

I have no hesitation in admitting that rolling power cuts are part of daily life in India, but we must also accept that energy production can fall far short of the demands of a fast-growing economy and an increasingly affluent population. India, by 2012, had an installed power capacity of 205,000 MW, about 35 per cent more than what it had five years earlier, thanks to the aggressive approach I had adopted. However, it was still only at about one-fifth of China's capacity. The gap between supply and demand remained, with the peak-hour deficit reaching about 10 per cent.

Often, the power shortage becomes more acute because of weak monsoons in agricultural states, such as Punjab and Uttar Pradesh. With less rain to irrigate crops, more farmers resort to drawing water from wells using electric pumps. High consumption of heavily subsidized diesel by farmers and businesses fuelled a gaping fiscal deficit that the Manmohan Singh government had vowed to tackle to restore confidence in the economy. But then, reducing subsidies is a politically difficult move.

My tenure at the power ministry, which started towards the end of the Tenth Plan period and covered the entire period for the Eleventh Plan (2007–2012), saw an additional generation of 80,000 MW, which was a record. The Eleventh Plan period alone saw an addition of 55,000 MW, which was two-and-a-half times the capacity addition during the Eighth, Ninth and Tenth Plan periods.

Of the five Ultra Mega Power Projects of 4,000 MW that I set up in India, two were coal pithead-based plants and three were coastal plants based on imported coal. The Power Finance Corporation was encouraged to establish transactional vehicles specifically to set up these projects, and obtain all the necessary regulatory clearances and fuel linkages. I also invited huge private investments in these companies, including from the United States of America. The whole process of selecting private investors in these companies was completed in a record time, though that also meant I had to often travel to America and other countries, such Denmark, Russia, Turkey, Tajikistan and Canada, in search of foreign direct investment (FDI).

ENVIRONMENT AND ECOLOGICAL BALANCE

In my opinion, India's path of development is based on both its unique resource endowments as well as the underlying premise of using every resource efficiently and sustainably. Rapid economic growth and poverty eradication have been our twin goals, along with our deep belief and adherence to our civilizational legacy, which places the highest value on the environment and the maintenance of the ecological balance. For us, sustainable development is an article of faith and what we have always sought to do is use all available energy resources towards the well-being of the people—a large percentage of whom have no access to commercial energy. Enhancing energy supply and access has, therefore, been a key component of our national development strategy.

This is what I had said in a speech at the 'Green India Summit' at the US Chamber of Commerce in October 2008. I won't reproduce the speech verbatim because fifteen years have passed and a lot of changes have happened since. What I'll do, instead, is try and condense what I told the summit held in Washington DC.

In my address, I noted that India was one of the first developing countries to have achieved the unique distinction of successfully decoupling economic growth from energy use:

> The IEA [International Energy Agency] publication of 2008 brings out clearly that India, with an energy intensity of 0.14 tonnes of oil equivalent is comparable with the advanced countries, and is better than China and other

> developing countries. Despite this, India has taken a proactive approach to further improve efficiency both in energy demand and down the supply chain. Special efforts are being made for the development of renewables and promotion of energy efficiency.

I told the audience that the new Electricity Act, enacted in the year 2003 required that distribution companies must buy a part of their total electricity from renewable sources. 'The regulators also give preferential prices for power from renewable sources. Over the past few years, this has resulted in the addition of … renewable-electricity capacity.'

CLEAN AND RENEWABLE ENERGY SOURCES

Speaking on clean and renewable energy, I said that India was the fourth-largest wind power producer in the world and added that our national policy placed the highest priority on the development of 'all possible potential of hydroelectricity', which was a clean and renewable source of energy.

The share of hydropower in India, during my time as power minister, rose to 36,000 MW, and we would add about 16,500 MW more of hydropower annually over the next few years. I also got the Union cabinet to approve that every family affected by a hydropower project would receive 100 units of free electricity per month for the next ten years. This was meant to ensure that the project-affected families had an assured revenue stream as well as tangible long-term benefits arising from a project for which they may have lost some land or faced hardships.

Speaking on nuclear energy, I said it accounted for less than 3 per cent of the domestic capacity but constituted an important component of India's energy mix in the future.

> We have made significant advances in our domestic three-stage nuclear programme. The historic India–US civil nuclear initiative, which has enabled India to resume nuclear commerce with the United States and other countries, will give a major boost to India's nuclear energy programme and, therefore, our ability to reduce our dependence on fossil fuel. Through international cooperation and domestic development, nuclear energy could meet as much as 20 per cent of the energy demand in India by 2050, adding potentially tens of thousands of megawatts of nuclear energy capacity in the country.

My speech also dwelt on the link between sustainable and accelerated economic growth, and commensurate growth in demand for energy.

> This demand for growth has had an adverse effect on the energy security of the country, not only due to the price volatility in the oil and gas market but also on account of supply constraints. Energy conservation is a vital policy tool in our quest to promote energy efficiency as a cost-effective and environmentally benign supplement to the overall energy sector strategy.

> We are striving to reduce the energy intensity of the economy by using a combination of appropriate regulatory frameworks, leadership and best-practice emulation programmes, and outreach and awareness campaigns. The Government of India is committed to the pursuit of our quest towards evolving a credible and sustainable national energy efficiency and conservation agenda, and thereby stimulating market transformation in favour of energy-efficient technologies and products.

The latest in our series of efforts, I said, included Prime Minister Manmohan Singh's pronouncement of the National Action Plan on Climate Change, which had identified eight missions, including the National Mission for Enhanced Energy Efficiency. The intention was to initiate a result-oriented and time-bound mechanism for achieving the objective of sustainable and rapid economic growth, along with effectively dealing with the global threat of climate change. The Action Plan had scaled up the energy-efficiency efforts on a mission mode and we had set ourselves an ambitious target of achieving savings of 5 per cent of energy consumption by way of energy-conservation measures.

A National Solar Mission had also been launched as part of the National Action Plan on Climate Change to significantly increase the share of solar energy in the total energy mix, while also recognizing the need to expand the scope of other renewable and non-fossil options, such as nuclear energy, wind energy and biomass. India is a tropical country, where sunshine is available for longer hours during the day and in great intensity. I said:

Solar energy, therefore, has great potential as a future energy source. It also has the advantage of permitting decentralized distribution of energy, thereby empowering people at the grassroots level. Photovoltaic cells are becoming cheaper with new technology. There are newer, reflector-based technologies that could enable setting up megawatt-scale solar power plants across the country.

Today, the world faces the reality of global warming, and its impact would not be an isolated occurrence confined to the countries that have contributed towards accumulating the carbon footprint but the future of the entire planet is at stake and successful resolution of this crisis would largely depend on how we globally tackle this challenge … India has taken a major lead in participating in the Clean Development Mechanism (CDM) programme and is diligently pursuing, in partnership with the United States and other countries, the goal for cleaner environment through the Asia Pacific Partnership on Climate Change and Development. India is also an active member of the Carbon Sequestration Leadership Forum. We are the first partner of the United States in the development of near emission-free power from coal in the Future Gen Project.

MAKING A POINT ON CARBON CAPTURE AND STORAGE

I told many international power experts that a populous country like India would not take up carbon capture and storage schemes at such an early stage in the development of this technology.

While we were willing to participate in any R&D on carbon capture and storage, unless the commercial viability of the technology was fully established and its safety features amply proved, it would just not be appropriate for India to take up such a project. I am happy to note that now, the Government of India has committed to reducing CO2 emissions by 50 per cent by 2050 and reaching net zero by 2070.

India is the third-largest emitter of CO2 in the world after China and the USA, with estimated annual emissions of about 2.6 gigatonnes per annum (GTPA). As a recent NITI Aayog report has acknowledged, even if India can substantially green the grid and meet the target of 500 GW of installed capacity of renewables by 2030, there would still be a need to meet the baseload power demand from fossil fuels (most likely coal) or other dispatchable sources, given the intermittency and non-dispatchable nature of solar and wind power.

I wrapped up my speech by highlighting my firm belief that cleaner power development technologies must be developed and shared through international cooperation.

> If we believe that climate change is a genuine global concern, we should not leave the dispersal and proliferation of cleaner energy technologies to market forces and commercial interest alone. If we trust so implicitly in the market, clean technologies will not be affordable or accessible to those countries and people, who need energy the most and are the fastest growing. The theme of this Conference should be interdependence, and we must

make the common development and sharing of cleaner technology a major recommendation if we are to sincerely pursue economic development with environmental protection. The developed countries should contribute to sustainable development of the world by providing the requisite funding support for the development of cleaner technologies in the public domain and for their adoption in the developing countries.

Dear readers, that concludes the section on my political and other important roles that came my way, sometimes in the most unexpected manner. As already mentioned, my term as Union power minister ended in July 2012. My next and final assignment at the Centre would be as the country's home minister, which I've already covered in the opening chapters.

The narrative now takes a break from chronology to return to a time when I was still a greenhorn in politics, a young man learning the ropes from those with greater experience, or mentors, as they say. The next section—Mentors and Leaders—is about my interactions with some key persons who helped shape my life and career, for better or for worse. And that section has to begin with the man who brought me into politics: Sharad Pawar. Back then, to those long-gone days.

SECTION VII

Mentors and Leaders

19

Sharad Pawar, the Pragmatist

'Ideologies contain in varying propositions, elements of explanation of fact and history, justification of demands and the faith in the ultimate truth or rightness of their case. They perform the triple function of simplifying, demanding and justifying.'

—C.B. Macpherson[20]

SHARAD PAWAR HAS been the most consummate politician, friend, mentor and colleague I have ever known—all rolled into one. It wouldn't be an exaggeration to say that my life and politics have been largely shaped by him, and I am indebted to him in more ways than I can ever acknowledge. For decades, I have been a beneficiary of his affection, largesse and support. Our destiny in the political arena criss-crossed on numerous occasions, often putting me in awkward and tricky situations where intrigue and doublespeak cast their shadows. But those fleeting spells of political opportunism could

20 C.B. Macpherson, *Democratic Theory: Essays in Retrieval* (Canada: OUP, 2014), 157–8.

not harm our bond. I remained wedded to my ideology and Pawar understood me well each time we found ourselves on opposite ends of the political spectrum. For a more discerning reader, it might seem a bit odd but, in Maharashtra politics, a cordial relation among political opponents has a rich, formidable and proud legacy.

My respect for Pawar 'saheb', as he is popularly known—a title he has not inherited but earned through respect, élan and a proven track record—went up several notches after seeing him stitch together the Maha Vikas Aghadi (MVA) coalition between the Congress, NCP and the Shiv Sena (Udhav) in 2019, and the way he stood for certain values after a split in his own party in 2023. That is the reason I leaned on Canadian political scientist C.B. Macpherson's words at the beginning of this chapter. For Pawar, political ideology has always been driven, and defined, by the need of the hour, and the demand for explanation and justification.

The day of 28 November 2019 was a significant one in the history of the Indian National Congress. It was the day we joined a government in Maharashtra headed by the Shiv Sena. The Congress's decision to support the Shiv Sena was not an easy one. Initially, Sonia Gandhi, Rahul Gandhi, A.K. Antony, Dr Manmohan Singh, Bhupesh Baghel—the Chhattisgarh chief minister—and a range of other party leaders were 'instinctively' opposed to it. But Pawar and some of us from Maharashtra had passionately argued in favour, recalling that during 1979–80, when Indira Gandhi and Sanjay Gandhi were out of power, the Congress had adopted a pragmatic approach to seek friendship with Balasaheb Thackeray, who incidentally had supported the Emergency. We also pointed out that while the Sena, since its inception, has been a chauvinistic and boisterous party, it was not a Sangh *parivar* affiliate like the Hindu Mahasabha, Bharatiya Jana Sangh, Ram Rajya Parishad, Bajrang Dal or the Vishwa Hindu Parishad.

Pawar's line of pragmatism gained momentum. He also repeatedly pointed out that as separate political entities, the Congress, Sena and his own Nationalist Congress Party would continue to have the freedom to profess and practise their core ideology. This nuanced distinction provided stability to the Udhav Thackeray ministry until unethical machinations led to its downfall. The MVA, however, stayed on politically.

In my assessment, Pawar decided to oppose the BJP because the voting pattern among Marathas has so far been a mixed one, with more voting against the BJP than for it in western Maharashtra. In fact, Maratha antipathy towards the BJP has been the only reason Pawar himself never tilted towards the party, despite overtures from Narendra Modi and others. The saddest part of betrayal, as Pawar may have realized, is that it never comes from your enemies.

In 2023, Pawar once again stood like a rock in the face of nefarious attempts to break his party. To this day, he remains a war horse, and we have reasons to feel proud and be inspired by his presence.

STUDENT LEADER

I had heard of Sharad Pawar when I was a law student in Pune. I had been looking for an opportunity to involve myself in student activism and was impressed by Pawar, who was then at the centre of the student movement in Pune. He was contesting from Baramati in the Assembly elections of 1967, when former chief minister Y.B. Chavan asked him to induct some fresh blood into the party organization. Pawar had zeroed in on me, Govindrao Adik, Mulchand Gothi, Eknath Salve, Dhairyasheel Pawar and Vinayakrao Patil.

When I met him for the first time, Pawar said he had a special admiration for me because of the way I had come up in life. I met him again when I was in the police. Then, one day, he asked me to consider resigning from the police force. He promised to take up my case for a ticket in the Assembly elections of 1972. I was married and had a daughter, so I was naturally hesitant to take the plunge.

The central leadership in Delhi did not clear my nomination, as I mentioned previously. I recall Pawar being somewhat apologetic because I had resigned from a secure job at his insistence. However, I held no grudges because I had no doubt that he had tried his best. I had seen him take up my case with Chandra Shekhar, a prominent Young Turk of that era, to intercede on my behalf. I later learnt that it was Babu Jagjivan Ram's preference for Tayappa Hari Sonawane that went against me. Pawar had narrated verbatim what Chandra

Shekhar-ji had told him: 'Sorry, I could not [manage a ticket for] that promising Dalit fellow you had recommended.'

I was disappointed but valued Pawar's affection for me much more than such temporary setbacks. He would later tell an interviewer, Dilip Chaware: 'I did not know how to face Shinde. I knew he would be waiting at Bombay airport for the list of candidates like many other aspirants. On the flight to Bombay, I could not think of anything else. In fact, my eyes filled with tears when I alighted from the plane and saw an eager Shinde in the crowd. Still trying to control my emotions, I broke the bad news to him. His reaction was touching.'

'[He said,] "Please don't feel so bad,"' Pawar told Chaware, narrating how I had responded. '"We will keep on working."'

Having failed to get the party ticket, I started practising law. Pawar subsequently appointed me as secretary of the Congress Forum for Socialist Action, and started taking me on tours and campaigns. I could sense that he was keeping a close tab on me, often watching how I interacted with party workers and the public in general. Neither of us knew that I would be contesting an election not too far away in the future.

The opportunity arose because of an unfortunate reason, when Sonawane passed away in 1974, necessitating a by-poll. Pawar swung into action. He first cleared my name from the state party unit and then sought Chandra Shekhar's help. This time, there was no resistance, even from Babu Jagjivan Ram. I was in the fray.

But there was another problem: finances. Pawar would solve that too. When I approached him saying I had no money or resources to fight the Assembly by-election, he quickly mobilized Rs 15,000, which was a fortune to me. He even assigned party veteran Namdeorao Jagtap to run my campaign.

I have no shame and hesitation in admitting that I was a complete greenhorn in politics. Pawar guided me, often placing a Gandhi cap on my head while on a campaign trail, teaching me how to wave at crowds and fold my hands to do namaste each time I faced a group of supporters or a large gathering. Naturally, I consider him as my mentor and worthy of the 'saheb' honorific, although we are almost of the same age.

After the elections were over and I had won, Jagtap submitted a detailed account of expenses and returned Rs 4,500 as unutilized funds. That was the level of probity and accountability prevalent in the Congress.

Pawar may not say it, but I owed my first ministerial assignment to him—though he worked his influence through former freedom fighter and party veteran Prabhakar Kunte, who told me that being a minister was the best way to serve the people in a parliamentary form of democracy. Pawar then urged Y.B. Chavan to have a word with Chief Minister V.P. Naik to induct me as a junior minister.

By 1979, I was labour minister with cabinet rank in the Sharad Pawar-led PDF government, a post that would teach me a lot about handling tricky situations. One such situation arose when some trade union leaders demanded that the Bombay

Industrial Relations (BIR) Act be scrapped. Pawar told me that if the demand was conceded, the city's textile mills and the Brihanmumbai Electricity Supply and Transport (BEST) undertaking would face closure. He suggested that I keep the issue pending while engaging in deliberations with various trade union leaders. Some of these exasperated leaders even reached out to Pawar to complain that 'the minister only laughs, he does not deliver'. Pawar, however, kept faith in me, and together we averted changes in the BIR Act. Pawar later told me he had studied my performance as a minister and sensed that I had the traits of a parliamentarian too.

By 1980, Indira-ji was back as Prime Minister and the Pawar ministry had been dismissed. I had a strong urge to join her but, at the same time, I did not want to disappoint Y.B. Chavan and Pawar. As the days passed, the internal turmoil became unbearable. Finally, I mustered the courage to speak to Pawar. Much to my surprise and relief, he was extremely understanding. He told me that my decision to join Indira-ji wouldn't hurt our personal ties. Decades later, when Pawar left the Congress on the grounds of Sonia Gandhi's foreign origins, I told him—in private, but firmly—that he was making a big mistake.

I value Pawar's magnanimity. Today, we have third-generation ties and our families are together on all important occasions.

WHEELS OF POLITICS

Pawar returned to the Congress when Rajiv Gandhi was the Prime Minister and, in June 1988, assumed charge as chief minister for the second time. In March 1990, he would be sworn in for the third time after the Assembly elections that year. But the wheels of politics turn on their own, and a tricky situation would arise because of political differences between Rajiv Gandhi and then Prime Minister Chandra Shekhar, who headed a minority government with outside support from the Congress. The Congress had many reasons to be dissatisfied with his government and, within my party, some leaders had reportedly informed Rajiv Gandhi that Pawar was tacitly helping his friend Chandra Shekhar.

Suddenly, four Maharashtra state ministers—Vilasrao Deshmukh, Ramrao Adik, Javed Khan and Surupsingh Naik—issued a statement against Pawar. I was then state Congress president and busy with my daughter's wedding. I must admit that erroneously, I had signed the paper as requested by Deshmukh. I realized my folly, but the deed was done.

Opponents of Pawar called a press conference at the residence of Deshmukh, who, as I have mentioned earlier, was also a close friend of mine. The ministers demanded that Pawar be sacked, and the move appeared poised for certain success as it was backed by former chief minister S.B. Chavan and Congress spokesperson V.N. Gadgil.

The revolt obtained legitimacy when I became its mascot and my official Pedder Road residence, 'Ryle Stone', became the operational headquarters of the pro-change front. Since S.B. Chavan and Gadgil too were openly demanding a change at the top, Pawar's position had become extremely vulnerable. He was under attack for the de-reservation of 285 strategic land properties from the development plan for Mumbai. There was unanimity that Pawar must go and, amid speculation about his possible successor, my name kept coming up.

But the seasoned politician that he was, Pawar had silently activated his counter-moves. What transpired between him and Rajiv Gandhi became public much later, when Pawar told an interviewer that Rajiv-ji had told the rebels to 'give Pawar a shake, not pull him down'. As no signal came from Delhi, the anti-Pawar camp grew restless and the state leaders started disassociating themselves from the revolt one by one. It was embarrassing for me as I was the Maharashtra Pradesh Congress Committee (MPCC) president.

The rebellion ended on the fifth day. Pawar reinstated all the rebel ministers in his cabinet on Rajiv Gandhi's suggestion but insisted on my removal as MPCC chief, arguing that an impression would be created that the Congress had wanted his removal. Pawar's condition was accepted. Rajiv Gandhi had realized that the party could not afford to antagonize a senior and ambitious leader like Pawar, especially when it was not in power at the Centre. Instead of losing a state and allowing the party to break up, Rajiv-ji felt that it would be better to take a step back and remove me from the post of PCC chief.

As things turned out, I not only lost the PCC chief's post but also the guardianship of Solapur. As if to rub salt into my wounds, my opponent, Vijaysinh Mohite-Patil, became the new guardian of Solapur.

In June 1991, P.V. Narasimha Rao took over as the Prime Minister and appointed Pawar as defence minister. Pawar's disciple, Sudhakar Rao Naik, succeeded him as the chief minister of Maharashtra and I felt an opportunity had eluded me. I also found myself being harassed for no reason. Naik had entrusted me with law and judiciary in addition to the urban development portfolio. The flashpoint was a sudden strike by lawyers in Mumbai. After conferring with all sides, I prepared a draft agreement, which Naik endorsed. In the final round, prior to calling off the strike, the protesting lawyers were to meet the chief minister and the chief justice. I had a prior commitment in Latur and asked the chief minister if I could stay away from Mumbai, which he permitted. The negotiations took place in Mumbai and the strike was called off, but Naik asked the governor to divest me of the law and judiciary portfolio. Many senior leaders, including Ramrao Adik, Shivajirao Patil Nilangekar, Vilasrao Deshmukh and Jawaharlal Darda, questioned the chief minister's action. When I called on Naik and tried to ascertain the reason, he was evasive and told me that it was the chief minister's prerogative to assign or take away portfolios.

But sentiments against Naik were becoming more and more vocal, and the government appeared to be in a crisis. Prime Minister Narasimha Rao was worried about the political instability and the AICC general secretary, Janardhan Poojary, was rushed to Mumbai to resolve the stalemate. I got back the portfolio.

Between 1992 and 2003, I did not hold any ministerial posts. In between, I led several parliamentary delegations abroad and was kept busy as a general secretary in charge of important states, including Bihar and Madhya Pradesh. In fact, Pawar, who was defence minister in the Rao government till March 1993, told an interviewer that he had recommended my name as AICC general secretary.

After the 1992 riots in Mumbai, the Maratha lobby got an opportunity to target Chief Minister Naik, who belonged to the Banjara community. There was talk that a backward caste leader should be replaced by another backward caste leader. People knew I was close to Sonia Gandhi and some even congratulated me, but I knew I wouldn't become chief minister.

Not yet.

20

Y.B. Chavan, a Man I Admired

RIGHT FROM MY college days, I was a huge admirer of Yashwantrao Balwantrao Chavan and fancied myself as a follower. Not only was he the first leader to take me under his wing, but he also told Sharad Pawar to look out for me when I was still in college in Pune. Son of a court bailiff, Chavan had risen from humble roots—something I found to be a common link between us.

Y.B. Chavan was a great orator, and always spoke with poise, dignity and a sense of authority—invariably holding people's attention when he addressed them. Well-versed with the ground situation, he loved interacting with people and did so with ease. Throughout his long and distinguished public career, he cared for the poor and for people from the backward classes. He was secular in his approach too. But it was his pragmatism and intellectual heft that drew me towards him. That is why I consider him as a mentor.

I can never forget how Chavan saheb helped me in the first election that I fought in 1974. His endorsement of my candidature had virtually evaporated the opposition within the Congress and a veteran like Namdeorao Jagtap had taken it upon himself to run my campaign.

A graduate in history and political science from Bombay University in pre-independent India, Chavan's command over English was excellent, as were his writings. While his canvas of thoughts and vision was nationalistic, he was, at the same time, an authority on international issues and could speak extensively on various subjects.

But Chavan saheb wasn't merely well educated; he used his learning to think about ways to improve the lives of ordinary folks. An advocate of social democracy, he never left the side of farmers and the poor. From the farming community himself, he was instrumental in establishing co-operatives in Maharashtra for the betterment of farmers. To my mind, he had all the qualities needed to become a Prime Minister, but unfortunately, his last important assignment was as the country's deputy PM in the short-lived Charan Singh government. Chavan saheb held many important ministerial portfolios, both at the state level and at the Centre, where he was in a league of his own, serving as defence minister, home minister, finance minister and external affairs minister—apart from being deputy PM—during an extended run that started from November 1962.

Earlier, in 1952, he was appointed minister of civil supplies, social welfare and forests by Morarji Desai, who was the chief minister of Bombay State. Chavan succeeded Desai as chief minister in 1956 after the latter moved to the Centre to become a minister in Jawaharlal Nehru's cabinet.

During his six years as chief minister—first of Bombay State and then of the newly carved out Maharashtra that came into existence on 1 May 1960—Chavan saheb created a niche for himself, focusing on sugar refining and the farm sector across all the regions of the state. Another legacy of his was adopting a cooperative approach to production and distribution. Landmark laws were passed under his watch, including an act that decentralized local government bodies and placed limits on the amount of agricultural land an individual could own. To me, Chavan saheb was the architect of modern Maharashtra.

In 1962, Nehru-ji appointed Chavan saheb as the country's new defence minister after V.K. Krishna Menon resigned over India's reverses in the brief Sino–Indian War. As defence minister, Chavan would see another war—with Pakistan—when Lal Bahadur Shastri was the Prime Minister. Chavan saheb also holds the distinction of getting elected to the Lok Sabha unopposed from Nashik in 1963. Then, in 1966, Indira-ji appointed him as Union home minister.

When his biography was released, Chavan saheb did not forget to send an invite to his ardent follower. I was the chief guest at that event. Looking back, I can say with confidence that Chavan saheb had the greatest influence on my life and I owe virtually everything to him.

21

My Friend Balasaheb Thackeray

ALTHOUGH A CONTROVERSIAL figure in Indian politics, Balasaheb Thackeray had a soft corner for me. This, perhaps, explains why I am talking about my relationship with the late Shiv Sena leader with a sense of nostalgia. Of course, this has nothing to do with his brand of politics; it is an entirely personal response.

It was just after I had joined politics and was part of Sharad Pawar's inner circle when I met Thackeray for the first time. While many other leaders distanced themselves from him for various reasons, I remained a friend of the Sena chief. Thackeray perhaps understood my feelings and often reciprocated in his characteristic style. He would often acknowledge, publicly, that I had been unfairly denied the chief ministership because I was a Dalit, despite being the most suitable for the job.

I still remember an incident that, if nothing else, showed Thackeray's sensitivity that not many politicians from a rival camp may have been capable of. That was a time when our parties were headed for a tussle against each other in an election. I was contesting against the Sena–BJP's candidate, and Thackeray had come to Solapur to campaign for the alliance. I wanted to meet him and he, too, I guess, had similar feelings. So, I went to his suite, hoping against hope that no mediaperson would be there. When I reached, I saw television crews adjusting their equipment. Thackeray noticed that the media photographers were zooming in on me. Another leader might have caused havoc by making me stand by his side for a photograph, but Thackeray told the journalists not to film us together, lest someone misused the visuals for political purposes.

There were quite a few raised eyebrows when Thackeray attended my daughter's wedding at Mahalaxmi Race Course. The Sena–BJP alliance was in power then. That was Thackeray's first public appearance since his wife Meena's death in 1995.

In 2003, when I contested an Assembly by-election to validate my stay in office after I had finally been appointed chief minister, the Sena offered the Solapur constituency on a platter by choosing not to contest. Nobody bought Thackeray's argument that he was not interested in the by-election because the term of the winner would be a short one (twenty-one months, as it turned out).

I must clarify here that I was not the only Congress leader in Thackeray's good books. The Sena supremo had good relations with Vasantdada Patil, too, among others.

Thackeray began his career as a cartoonist. He formed the Shiv Sena in 1966 at the age of forty while working as a cartoonist for the *Free Press Journal* in Mumbai. This was a time when migrants from south Indian states, particularly Tamil Nadu, were calling the shots in the metropolis and many Marathi-speaking youths—'sons of the soil'—were unable to find employment. On the political front, communists and labour unions were becoming increasingly dominant.

Before becoming a full-time politician, Thackeray had left his job to start *Marmik*, a satirical weekly. *Marmik* would highlight the recruitment of non-Maharashtrians in both government and private industries under the headline '*Vaacha ani gappa basa*', or 'Read and keep quiet'. Soon, people from south India were targeted with the war cry, '*Bajao pungi, bhagao lungi*', which Thackeray had coined, playing on sartorial habits and preferences from southern states, particularly Tamilians.

Although I had cordial relations with Thackeray, I could never justify his politics or the tools he had adopted. He had a sharp tongue too and used to be strident in his views about Muslims in public, but this much I can say: He was different in private. One of my bodyguards was a Muslim and Balasaheb cared a lot about him.

Balasaheb's son, Uddhav Thackeray, has taken his father's legacy forward but will take time to learn. As for the Congress, it had always opposed the Shiv Sena's communal views, but I think the Congress–Sena (MVA) alliance was necessary, and I see a fruitful partnership between the Sena, Congress and the NCP. The MVA alliance also led to a softening of the Sena's Hindutva plank. As far as I am concerned, it was an astute political move.

22

Some Other Key Figures

IN MY DECADES-LONG career in politics, there have been many, in addition to the ones discussed hitherto, who played a role, if not central then certainly more than peripheral, in my unexpected ascent to the highest echelons of the government. A fair assessment would be that I learnt from each of these leaders in the same way a student learns from various teachers, consciously or unconsciously, imbibing values and assimilating ideas to be retrieved later in life and put to use when circumstances demanded it. This chapter is dedicated to some of those leaders I came across in my political journey and who shaped my thinking in some way or the other. It also includes those with whom I had ideological and political differences. Because, in sum and substance, I have never considered my political adversaries to be my enemies.

VASANTDADA PATIL

Vasantdada Patil was a freedom fighter. Although many consider him a Gandhian, I feel he was deeply influenced by Netaji Subhas

Chandra Bose too. In our personal conversations, Vasantdada would often say that by themselves, neither satyagraha nor *morchas* nor people's movements would have got us freedom, and the role of our brave revolutionaries who carried out daring attacks on public utilities, including train robberies, to provide the money to keep the struggle alive remained understated. He himself was involved in procuring firearms from Goa.

During the Raj, many criminal cases were filed against him and the British government even offered a bounty of Rs 1,000 for any information leading to his capture. Sent to jail in Sangli, where he was from, Vasantdada was badly injured while trying to escape. Shot in the shoulder, he carried the bullet lodged inside his body as a badge of honour.

After Independence, Vasantdada worked silently among the masses, adhering to Gandhian principles as he went about improving the lot of farmers. In 1960, he started an industrial society to increase irrigation in Sangli and became the chief promoter of the Groundnut Processors' Cooperative Society to promote collective local income methods.

When Vasantdada became chief minister for the second time in 1983, one of the portfolios he handed me was finance, although I had no formal background or training in financial matters. I would also remember him as someone who piloted a bill to create private engineering and technical colleges in Maharashtra, making our state a centre for engineering and technical education.

Vasantdada's ties with the Indian National Congress remained intact till his last days, though he fought many battles within the Congress *parivar*. He was briefly a general secretary for the party, but his heart was with Maharashtra and its people. Loyal to the state, party and the country, Vasantdada was a visionary who believed in bringing about change through better access to education, value to farmers and political acknowledgement of the people. A recipient of the Padma Bhushan in 1967, he continues to live in the heart of every Marathi who looks back with pride at the glorious young days of the state.

V.P. NAIK

Vasantrao Phulsingh Naik was from a prosperous farming family belonging to the Banjara community in the eastern Yavatmal district. He was chief minister of Maharashtra for a little over eleven years, from December 1963 to February 1975. Like many others, he too had been mentored by Y.B. Chavan. Earlier, Naik had also served as a minister in what was then known as Madhya Bharat, which was later merged with Madhya Pradesh.

I became a minister for the first time when Naik was chief minister of Maharashtra. Chief ministers seldom campaigned in by-elections in those days, but Naik came for mine, telling me that he had made an exception because he thought I was a promising candidate with a bright future.

When Naik headed the Maharashtra government, the communists wielded a lot of influence in the state. In her work on Balasaheb Thackeray, *Hindu Hriday Samrat*, author-journalist Sujata Anandan has meticulously recorded how the Congress used the Shiv Sena to 'fix' the communists and a range of other players. She also writes that the Shiv Sena, in its nascent days, was derogatorily referred to as 'Vasant Sena' on account of Naik's alleged tacit support. I don't know to what extent Naik had supported the Sena, but I can say that whatever happened was for the good of Maharashtra.

I was present in Mumbai when President Pranab Mukherjee was the chief guest at an event that brought the curtains down on celebrations to mark one hundred years of Naik's birth. At the concluding ceremony held in July 2013 at the TIFR auditorium in Colaba, Mukherjee said Naik boldly informed the Centre that five-year plans had no flexibility in implementation.

He was also spot on when he remarked, 'Naik headed a stable government in the era when the country was going through political turbulence ... Frequent elections were a routine phenomenon at the Centre, but Naik ruled a stable government for eleven years, and provided economic and political stability.'

When it was my turn to speak, I told the gathering that some of the political success I achieved was possible only because of Naik's guidance.

V.N. GADGIL

V.N. Gadgil was my teacher at the New Law College in Mumbai where I studied. Apart from being a Union minister, Gadgil was also a senior advocate in the Supreme Court, honorary professor of economics in Ruparel College, Mumbai, and professor of constitutional law in New Law College, Mumbai.

Despite his staunch stand against communalism in every form, Gadgil was a close friend of Balasaheb Thackeray. But, like me, he would also oppose him from time to time. Extremely well-read and articulate, Gadgil was considered a party ideologue and I made it a habit to closely follow his speeches in Parliament. He shared a great relationship with Sharad Pawar too.

Gadgil was general secretary of the Congress in the AICC and, when I went to Delhi for the first time for a party ticket, I stayed at his house. It was bitterly cold and his house was so crowded that there weren't enough blankets for everybody. So what we did was remove the curtains and use them as blankets. Gadgil was very accommodating and helped me get a ticket as well.

From 1971 to 1980, Gadgil was a Rajya Sabha MP; he then represented Pune in the Lok Sabha for several terms before returning to the Upper House in 1994, where he remained a member till 2000. He served as minister of state for defence and communications under Indira Gandhi, and later handled information and broadcasting when Rajiv Gandhi was the Prime Minister. He also served as Congress spokesperson under three party chiefs: Rajiv Gandhi, P.V. Narasimha Rao and Sitaram Kesri. Gadgil is credited with setting up the Indian Broadcasting (Programme) Service for national broadcasters Doordarshan and All India Radio.

When Gadgil passed away in 2001, President K.R. Narayanan paid a moving tribute to his personal friend: 'I mourn the death of a personal friend with whom I have had the occasion to interact closely for many years, and whose erudition and aesthetic sense I have admired.'

A.R. ANTULAY

AICC general secretary, Union minister, chief minister of Maharashtra—Abdul Rahman Antulay wore several hats during his career in politics. A staunch supporter of both Indira Gandhi and Sanjay Gandhi, he remained so throughout the Emergency.

I once met Antulay at an airport; we had been called by Sonia Gandhi and Dr Manmohan Singh for ministerial positions. The next day, both of us took our oaths.

When I came into politics, Antulay, a barrister from Lincoln's Inn, was a minister in Maharashtra and would often take drastic action without considering the consequences. Nonetheless, he did good work for the poor and for minorities. As chief minister, he became famous for stepping out after midnight to keep an eye on the law-and-order situation. Among the initiatives he launched as chief minister were the Sanjay Gandhi Niradhar Yojana (a monthly financial aid scheme for the poor), and pension and housing facilities for legislators and media-persons.

As a minister in Narasimha Rao's cabinet, Antulay had stunned Congress leaders and workers by declaring himself a 'Shiv Sainik'. He even asked an interviewer not to address him as 'Abdul Rahman', saying he preferred to be called A.R. Antulay.[21]

Earlier, in 1982, as chief minister of Maharashtra, Antulay had sought an appointment with the Queen of England so that he could request her to return 'Bhawani', the sword that belonged to Chhatrapati Shivaji. The request, moved through the Indian mission in London, had resulted in Antulay getting an appointment; but he was unseated before his London visit.

21 'First victim of "scam" passes away', *The Telegraph*, 3 December 2014, https://www.telegraphindia.com/india/first-victim-of-scam-passes-away/cid/283900.

23

Sonia Gandhi, Who Always Trusted Me

THE FIRST TIME I met Sonia Gandhi was when Rajiv Gandhi had taken me along with him to America as a delegate to the United Nations, where I was asked to make a speech in the General Assembly. I could sense in our first meeting that Sonia-ji was not a very chatty person; she was measured, observant and courteous to a fault. In America, we used to have dinner meets, where I got plenty of opportunities to interact with her.

Over the years, I would often be in attendance when Rajiv-ji and Sonia-ji toured Maharashtra. But Sonia-ji stayed away from politics until 1997, and I never got to discuss active politics with her, though I was in Parliament and in the AICC secretariat as party general secretary.

In 1991, amid the hustle and bustle of upcoming parliamentary elections, Rajiv Gandhi had visited Solapur along with Sonia-ji. I had wanted them to camp at my farm bungalow, but Rajiv-ji did not accept the invitation due to paucity of time. When I offered him a couple of boxes of grapes grown on my farm, he sensed my disappointment and promised to stay there on his next visit to Solapur. He also told me that he had heard a lot about my 25-acre farm and its high-quality, seedless grapes from Balram Jakhar, a former Lok Sabha speaker and noted agriculturalist.

'Shinde-ji, Balram-ji has told me that your farm is very nice. I would love to come and see it,' he said.

I told him I would build a new, big guest house, especially for him.

My wife, Ujwala, had selected for Sonia-ji an exotic handwoven Solapur silk sari with floral motifs and a Paithani-design pallu. For anybody interested in the history of Paithani saris, named after Paithan town in Aurangabad district (officially known as Chhatrapati Sambhaji Nagar district now), these saris go back around 2,000 years. After a few days, Ujwala received a signed letter from Sonia Gandhi, thanking her for the sari. Unfortunately, Rajiv-ji's 'next visit' never happened—a suicide bomber from the Liberation Tigers of Tamil Eelam (LTTE) assassinated him as he campaigned in Sriperumbudur, Tamil Nadu—but Sonia-ji kept her late husband's word and stayed with us when she visited Solapur during the 2004 elections. I was chief minister of Maharashtra then and Sonia-ji, recalling Rajiv Gandhi's affection for me, stayed at our farmhouse.

As long as Sonia-ji stayed there, I didn't allow any reporter or press photographer inside our farmhouse. There was a threat to her life at that time, and I had also sensed that she was a very private person and I imagine she valued that discretion.

Reluctant to enter politics at first, she has since evolved into an astute leader—at home in a world of intrigues, where appearances are notoriously deceptive. To quote from *Macbeth*, it is a world where 'there's daggers in men's smiles'.

When I look back at the years that have gone by, one of my biggest takeaways has been Sonia-ji's trust and faith in an ordinary party worker like me. As I have noted earlier, her trust sustained me through disappointments and she made sure that I was never completely denied opportunities. I, for my part, have never revealed to anyone any conversation I have had with Sonia-ji in private and I intend to maintain that till I breathe my last—as a matter of both policy and principle.

That concludes the penultimate section of this book and it is, perhaps, entirely apt to end with Sonia Gandhi. If Sharad Pawar was my friend, mentor and colleague, who guided me through those initial years, Sonia-ji has been the rock whose unstinted support played a huge role in my career, which, I believe, has been reasonably successful.

Some of my readers might wonder why this chapter on Sonia Gandhi is so brief compared to the one on Pawar. My explanation is that this chapter is about my personal equation with Sonia-ji. The political part has already been dealt with in this back-and-forth narrative.

Let's now move on then to the next and final section: 'Recollections and Reflections'.

SECTION VIII

Recollections and Reflections

24
A Straight Path

WHILE SPEAKING AT a ceremony meant to felicitate him in June 2003 in Solapur, I had said that one criticism I often had to face was that my speeches were too inoffensive for a politician. Some have even used the word 'sugary' to describe them. It is too late in the day for me to go into whether such criticism was valid, but the way I see it, a leader must combine a soft tongue and be tough at the same time, without hurting anyone. That is an approach I have always taken and it has seldom let me down.

While on the topic of rulers, I am reminded of Niccolo Machiavelli's famous lion and fox metaphor that the Italian diplomat, author, and political theorist had come up with in his sixteenth-century political treatise, *The Prince*. The lion, Machiavelli had said, cannot protect itself from traps, while the fox cannot defend itself from wolves. One must, therefore, be a fox to recognize traps and a lion to frighten away the wolves.

What Machiavelli was effectively suggesting was that a ruler should be both brave like a lion and cunning like a fox.

I subscribe to the first part of this counsel. The ruler should be brave, but cunning towards whom? To the society, to the state? I don't think that's a very healthy approach. Leaders must certainly be brave, but they should also remember that their constituents—the people—are the real rulers in a democracy. A prince—or ruler—must serve and deliver, knowing full well that people would still be critical. What the ruler should do is take cognisance of people's views, learn from the media what the public is saying and introspect, rather than take offence. Our democracy will be successful only if we adopt this approach. Unfortunately, too often have I seen barbarism practised in the name of democracy.

Coming back to my long stint in politics, I have never been overwhelmed by any office I held, whether it was that of a chief minister or a governor. I have tried to maintain my equanimity and always kept this in mind: Society pays you in the same coin with which you serve it. It is this straight path that I have always followed—sincere hard work with the right intentions. And I have never shied away from taking on challenges. Indeed, I love accepting challenges and believe in what Molière, the seventeenth-century French playwright, had said many years ago, 'The greater the obstacle, the more glory in overcoming it.' It is not that I seek out challenges, but they have been a constant companion in my life.

THE GRAVEST CHALLENGES

A big challenge I faced in the first year of becoming Maharashtra's finance minister in the early eighties was a constitutional tangle.

An amendment to the Finance Bill passed by the legislature's upper chamber was ignored by the Lower House and the state's budget was passed without taking it into account. When the matter came up for discussion in the legislative council, my government had no satisfactory explanation. I had no choice but to call a special sitting of the Lower House to consider and reject the amendment.

But nothing could have prepared citizens for what happened on 12 March 1993, when a series of blasts tore through Mumbai, leaving more than 200 people dead and over a thousand injured. The blasts left people panic-stricken and police morale was at its lowest. I was a Rajya Sabha MP at that time and also an AICC general secretary but did not hold any ministerial position. That didn't deter me. As a former policeman, I confronted the challenge head-on and am happy to recollect that many perpetrators were rounded up within hours. The plot was aimed at shaking the confidence of the public and investors, creating an impression that Maharashtra and Mumbai were not safe.

Another challenge I faced was after I had taken over as chief minister of Maharashtra. I had been taking many crucial decisions for the have-nots and one of them was helping poor, elderly parents who had taken to begging after being driven out of their homes by their children. I had come up with a scheme called the Indira Gandhi Women's Protection Scheme to provide shelter for such women but ran into a lot of resistance. Despite having the image of a jolly fellow (*hansmukh*), I stood by my decision. More than one lakh women across the state benefited from the scheme in the first year of its implementation. Another initiative, the Chief Minister's Career Guidance Scheme, was born out of my own experience. When I was a student there was no formal system in place to offer career guidance.

A litmus test I faced within days of taking over as chief minister in January 2003 was when social crusader Anna Hazare started a fast-unto-death, demanding action against some NCP ministers accused of irregularities. Neither was the crisis of my own making—it was a political crisis I had inherited—nor did I have the freedom to take action against ministers from a coalition partner. But I found a way out. The ministers submitted their resignations while a retired Supreme Court judge was appointed to probe the allegations. Although the crisis was defused, it left a bitter taste in many mouths.

As chief minister, I tried my best to prevail upon the BJP-led NDA government at the Centre to help Maharashtra in its hour of need. My demand was simple: The norms for financial assistance that applied to Odisha, Gujarat and Andhra Pradesh should be applicable in the case of Maharashtra too. It didn't happen, despite my repeated visits to Delhi. By the time I left office in 2004, Maharashtra had repaid over Rs 9,000 crore of its loans. The outcome was that the World Bank restored its financial assistance to the state.

BEST PARLIAMENTARIAN

I have had the privilege of serving in both Houses of Parliament and seeing up close the intricacies of national politics as they unfolded before me. The nineties were a particularly fraught period for the Congress, which was going through a crisis because of internal disquiet, the demolition of the Babri Masjid and the serial blasts in Mumbai. Then, by early 1996, many senior leaders and ministers had left the party over the controversial allegations in the Jain diaries. Serious allegations were levelled against Prime Minister Narasimha Rao too.

I had an opportunity to work closely with Rao and learnt how a seasoned leader dealt with difficult situations. I had never worked under Rajiv Gandhi but could well imagine the impact he must have had. Rao was a scholar and an accomplished writer. He had varied interests and, in Maharashtra, he was respected for his masterly translation of some classic works of Marathi literature into Telugu.

As a member of the Rajya Sabha, I raised several issues of national importance and would eventually be adjudged the best parliamentarian for the six years I was in the Upper House, from 1992 to 1998. My debut was through a calling attention motion concerning an atrocity in BJP-ruled Rajasthan where twelve Dalits were allegedly burnt to death. I had backed my speech with facts and figures, bringing to the Prime Minister's notice the rise in alleged atrocities against Dalits in BJP-ruled states. The speech was appreciated not only by my party president but also by Opposition leaders.

During my six years in the House, I asked hundreds of starred and un-starred questions, highlighting official apathy towards filling up vacancies in government posts reserved for the Scheduled Castes and Scheduled Tribes, and the failure to lift the poor above the poverty line. I moved fourteen private member's bills, effectively establishing that even a ruling party member could fight the system by remaining within limitations. On 9 March 1996, Mother Teresa felicitated me with the National Citizen Award for my parliamentary performance.

When I was removed from the post of Congress general secretary in the later part of 1990s, many people had said that my prospects had ended. But that interpretation was not correct as I handled many responsibilities later. I never sulked when I was not given a post.

'ZERO CLUB'

I like to remind everyone that I belong to what I call the 'Zero Club'. Members of this club are those who started their life with nothing but still rose high—much higher than they themselves would have ever thought they were capable of. I remember a memorable occasion in 2007 when an honorary DLitt (Doctor of Letters) was conferred on me by Padmashree D.Y. Patil University in Navi Mumbai. The chief guest at the programme was Dr Raghunath Mashelkar, who was president of the Indian National Science Academy, whom I aptly described as another member of the 'Zero Club'. As many readers would know, Dr Mashelkar is one of India's most eminent scientists. He is known for his contributions to India's National Chemical Laboratory and Council of Scientific and Industrial Research, for multiple 'Mashelkar Committees', and a successful campaign against foreign patents on Indian traditional knowledge. Dr Mashelkar, while addressing the gathering, recalled how his father had died when he was barely six. Though he ranked eleventh in the merit list of matriculation examination, Mashelkar's family could not afford to send him to a college. Scholarships came to his rescue and we gained a great scientist in him.

In the social surroundings in which I was brought up, the sole aim of the people around me was survival. They lived from hand to mouth, their horizon was limited, they had no motivation, no ambition to achieve anything and they were made to believe that their lives were purposeless. The pastime for children like me was to while away our days in vagrancy, skipping school, getting involved in gang fights and watching movies by sneaking into cinemas.

Like most Hindu households, my home too had a tradition of worship and my parents would fast on holy days. But the scriptures did not have a place in our home. Without any formal education, my parents were not too comfortable with the written word. But they made sure that I went to school so that I could get ahead in life. After my father's death, my link with education was broken, and though my mothers insisted I continue my studies, I resisted for some time. They did not lose patience and told me stories from mythology with invariably the same message: Share with others, worship your elders and serve the needy. This constant hammering in of ageless values finally changed me and I started taking an interest in studies again.

I sold incense sticks and toffees, and earned the confidence that hard work could support me. My various jobs brought me into contact with the outside world and my horizons began expanding. I realized the inherent limitations the archaic caste system had imposed upon a substantial chunk of the population—like me, who had the misfortune of being born low in the social hierarchy. This period taught me to question norms. Even now, I often ask myself why caste-based discrimination should exist if all Hindus belong to the same religion. I have no hesitation in pointing out that there are more inconsistencies than consistencies in our social and religious activities, and that compulsion is stronger than devotion.

People, including my friends and well-wishers, often ask me about the 'higher powers' that shaped my life. They want to know if some divine dispensation showered its blessings upon me, or if there was some magic that enabled a person born at the lowest rung of society to climb to such high positions of political authority. I tell them I have come to the conclusion that circumstances spurred me to shape my own life.

We often tend to give the entire credit for an individual's success to their destiny and a favourable alignment of stars, and, generally, don't like to accept that an individual can achieve success through hard work—though other factors may have been at play too. Consequently, we tend to see success as some kind of a mystery, while different people try in different ways to unravel this non-existent secret. There is no mystery in my life. Whatever little I have achieved is because of my drive to succeed. I am what I am, and all my achievements and failures are my own.

FAITH IN HUMANITY

I have been fortunate to meet many God-like people, but I have neither seen God nor has anyone shown God to me. So, by the time I was a young man, I had already concluded that concepts such as a divine boon or a guru's gift were all abstract ideas. It does not mean that I am a non-believer, but I shun superstition in all forms and manifestations. I abhor blind faith in religion and feel that such concepts restrict the potential of an individual, sow the seeds of doubt in their mind, shake their self-confidence and generally come in the way of personal development. Our failures lead us to justify our surrender to God, destiny and religion, and we try to find references in scriptures to rationalize this surrender and console ourselves.

God, religion and faith are, perhaps, inevitable in one's personal life, but they should not reflect in one's public life. I have faith in human beings and their capabilities: I believe that any individual can attain greatness, provided they are determined to achieve it. My life's journey is testimony to what can be achieved through determination and self-confidence. Instead of accepting things meekly, we should try to change the circumstances that hold us back.

I have never been a devotee of any guru or maharaj, but I have followed the example of certain people from whom I have learnt a lot. My mothers provided the foundation and later, my circumstances became my teacher. My interest in studying the Marathi language and political science cultivated my love for reading and exploring new subjects. Y.B. Chavan was my icon, and I would carefully listen whenever he spoke in public. In the world of the arts, my love for theatre and music provided an opportunity to get closer to great performers. Among my favourite singers and musicians are Lata Mangeshkar, Pandit Bhimsen Joshi, Mukesh, C. Ramachandra, and sitarist Abdul Halim Jaffer Khan.

I had no opportunity to get close to them in my early days, but I saluted their greatness from afar and cherished the qualities they displayed as public figures.

25

An Annual Ritual

FINALLY, I HAVE come to the last chapter of this book, exhausted by the effort but excited and a little nervous at the same time. Every writer, I guess, feels this way. Perhaps it has something to do with a sense of release and the realization that there's no turning back now—more so with autobiographies, which involve baring one's thoughts to an unknown number of complete strangers, without the cloak of invisibility that fiction writers have. Whether this book comes across as authentic, only my readers can say, but I have tried to be as candid as possible. And it is with the same candour that I intend to wrap up this narrative before I give myself up to the discernment of my readers.

This chapter is about a ritual I would observe unfailingly every year—a visit to a temple on a particular date.

Surprised? That this comes from someone who had only a few pages back spoken so emphatically about the primacy of individual agency? But, dear readers, if you notice carefully,

I have never in this narrative disputed the possibility that God might exist. I have merely said I haven't seen God, and that faith and religion should not intrude into the public domain. But God can certainly exist for us in our personal lives and, perhaps, inevitably so.

So, every year, I make it a point to visit the Mahalakshmi temple in Mumbai on 6 April. I walk up to a particular boulder through a maze of many such boulders along the shoreline that leads to the ancient abode of the goddess. I stand erect, close my eyes and then offer a few coins to the Arabian Sea, the imperturbable sentinel that has been witness to many crucial twists and turns in my life.

I generally reach the temple in the morning for the *aarti*. In 2006, I was unable to leave Delhi in time for the *aarti* because there was a European delegation in the capital to discuss some power projects. But as soon as the meeting was over, I caught a flight, performed the annual ritual and returned to Delhi the same night.

The first time I had gone there was in 1957, when I was a fatherless teen, depressed, defenceless and low on confidence—a situation exacerbated by my caste identity, which felt like a heavy weight around my neck. My mothers, both unlettered, struggled hard to make ends meet, and there was not enough to eat at home and no support to continue my education.

Then, one day, on the spur of the moment, I decided to come to Mumbai from Solapur and reached the vicinity of the temple, unsure where I was headed. In that frame of mind, I rested on the boulder and suddenly felt something hard against my big toe. I bent down, groped around in the water and caught hold of a paisa. Rather than taking it as a divine gift, I felt even more miserable, thinking that destiny was mocking me for not even having a paisa in my pocket. I gave the paisa to a beggar and walked away.

That day, in 1957, I had returned home to find the offer to join Solapur court as a *pattewala* (boy-peon) waiting for me. That would be a turning point in my life.

So many years have passed since, but I have neither forgotten that moment, that coin nor that beggar, nor failed to return to the boulder on 6 April every year, even if it is only for a few minutes.

About the Authors

Sushilkumar Shinde is a veteran politician who served as the Minister of Home Affairs (2012–14), Minister of Power (2006–12) and Leader of the House in the Lok Sabha (2012–2014). He served as the Chief Minister of Maharashtra from 2003 to 2004. As Maharashtra's finance minister, Shinde holds the record of presenting nine consecutive annual budgets in the state assembly.

Rasheed Kidwai is a journalist, author and political analyst. He is a visiting fellow at the Observer Research Foundation (ORF). Former associate editor at *The Telegraph*, Kidwai tracks government, politics, community affairs and Hindi cinema, and has written several books on these topics. A graduate of St. Stephen's College, Delhi University, he holds a master's degree in mass communication from Leicester University. He also contributes as a political analyst to News 18, ABP News, NDTV and India Today TV, among others.